apple pie

AN AMERICAN STORY

apple pie

AN AMERICAN STORY

John T. Edge

G. P. PUTNAM'S SONS

NEW YORK

G. P. Putnam's Sons
Publishers Since 1838
Published by the Penguin Group • Penguin Group (USA) Inc., 375 Hudson Street, New York,
New York 10014, USA • Penguin Group (Canada), 10 Alcorn Avenue, Toronto, Ontario,
Canada M4V 3B2 (a division of Pearson Penguin Canada Inc.) • Penguin Books Ltd, 80 Strand,
London WC2R 0RL, England • Penguin Ireland, 25 St Stephen's Green, Dublin 2, Ireland
(a division of Penguin Books Ltd) • Penguin Group (Australia), 250 Camberwell Road, Camberwell,
Victoria 3124, Australia (a division of Pearson Australia Group Pty Ltd) • Penguin Books India Pvt Ltd,
11 Community Centre, Panchsheel Park, New Delhi–110 017, India (a division of Penguin Group
Books India (P) Ltd) • Penguin Group (NZ), Cnr Rosedale and Airborne Roads, Albany, Auckland,
New Zealand (a division of Pearson New Zealand Ltd) • Penguin Books (South Africa) (Pty) Ltd,
24 Sturdee Avenue, Rosebank, Johannesburg 2196, South Africa

Penguin Books Ltd, Registered Offices: 80 Strand, London WC2R 0RL, England

Library of Congress Cataloging-in-Publication Data

Edge, John T.
Apple pie : an American story / John T. Edge.
p.   cm.
ISBN 0-399-15215-6
1. Pies—United States.   2. Cookery (Apples)   I. Title.
TX773.E334   2004   2004054463
641.8'652—dc22

Printed in the United States of America
1   3   5   7   9   10   8   6   4   2

This book is printed on acid-free paper. ∞

Photographs © 2004 Amy Evans
Book design by Stephanie Huntwork

While the author has made every effort to provide accurate telephone
numbers and Internet addresses at the time of publication, neither
the publisher nor the author assumes any responsibility for
errors, or for changes that occur after publication.

The recipes contained in this book are to be followed exactly as written. The
Publisher is not responsible for specific health or allergy needs that may
require medical supervision. The Publisher is not responsible for
any adverse reactions to the recipes contained in this book.

WITH LOVE FOR BLAIR, A NONPAREIL BAKER
AND THE MOST GENEROUS SOUL I KNOW

If I were to create a coat of arms for our country, a pie would be its heraldic symbol.

—*attributed to the figment known as Betty Crocker*

Contents

Series Introduction

This is the second in a series of books that celebrates America's iconic foods. Fried chicken led off. Hamburgers & French fries will come next. Then donuts. To my mind, these are small-d democratic foods that conjure our collective childhood and evoke the question once posed by a Chinese philosopher: "What is patriotism but nostalgia for the foods of our youth?"

I chose these foods because they transcend interregional variation and internecine debate over origins. Recognized from the Atlantic to the Pacific as uniquely American, they evoke the culinary and cultural fabric of our nation.

Though the places profiled and the recipes detailed can be read as keys to eating well here in the States, my intent was not to compile a list of the country's top bakers. Instead, please consider this to be my pilgrimage in search of America's gastronomic grail. In this book and the others that accompany it, I strive to introduce you to people and foods that make up a true American banquet.

In Pie We Trust

Writing about apple pie is a lazy man's pursuit. Rhapsodize about flaky crust and crisp yet unctuous apples, and before you know it you're halfway home. The rest comes naturally: Sketch scenes of pies cooling on windowsills. Stage a few Fourth of July interviews with pie-loving, baby-kissing politicians. Then trot out mom and cue the Don McLean album.

Cynical? Admittedly. *Truthful?* To a certain

extent. I've read something like sixteen pie books over the course of the past year. Memoirs, travel quests, cookbooks with pretensions: no matter their guise, far too many were all meringue, no filling. And I can't count how many newspaper and magazine articles I've perused wherein the author does nothing more than append his or her personal experience to a press release from the National Pie Council. (More on that august body later.)

I'm not saying that American letters is devoid of sober reflection on apple pie. And I'm not preaching that all writers need be sober. But I do believe that if apple pie is our national dessert—and who dares say it isn't?—then a writer in possession of intellect and a book contract is obliged to, at the very least, dig a bit deeper. How, why, and under what circumstances did apple pie come to be an artifact of American culture?

Of course, I am not the first author to lay claim to this territory—nor am I the ablest. In his 1987 book *Simple Cooking*, John Thorne suggested that our love of apple pie owes a debt to our familiarity with—and proximity to—local apple varieties. He even managed to bring his mother into the conversation without tipping toward syrupy recollection.

"Pick your apple tree and stick with it," he wrote. "My mother makes a great apple pie from the Wolf River apples that grow (and grew long before they ever got there) in the pasture of their old Maine farm. Hardly any source mentions the Wolf River; it is not so much rare as deliberately obscure, being not an immediately attractive apple. But it's there, fresh and free, so my mother has taken its measure, upping sugar and baking time when it's fresh and tart, and lowering both later, when it's neither. She knows that apple; this, not the apple, makes the difference."

Writing in 1976, on the occasion of our nation's bicentennial, M. F. K. Fisher tossed her fork down like a gauntlet. "It is as meaningless to say that something is 'as American as apple pie' as it is to assert that a Swedish or Irish grandfather who emigrated to Minnesota was a 'first American.' Both the pie and the parent sprang from other cultures, and neither got here before the Indian." Amidst the nationalistic bluster of the day, Fisher risked being dubbed a grouch, but she made her point—which was, if I may bastardize Socrates, that the unexamined pie is not worth eating.

Harriet Beecher Stowe, author of the 1852 abolitionist novel *Uncle Tom's Cabin,* also gave thought to apple pie's parentage—and the uniquely American character of its diffusion. Like Fisher, who eventually came around to the idea that modern apple pie is as distinctly American as any product of our culture, Stowe found a way to acknowledge foreign birth while simultaneously celebrating pie's Americanness. "The pie is an English institution," she wrote, "which, planted on American soil, forthwith ran rampant and burst forth into an untold variety of genera and species."

———

these words bookend our love affair with pie. Stowe wrote at a time when the intertwining of American identity and apple pie was inevitable but not yet manifest. Fisher and Thorne had the perspective of hindsight. By the time they sat down with pen and paper, apple pie identity was so well ingrained that enthusiasm was giving way to cynicism. In the epoch that spans that gap—roughly the mid-1800s through the early-to-middle 1900s—the myth was wrought. Here are a few of the cultural forces that *may* have played a role in the popularization of apple pie:

■ For much of our colonial history, we grew apples for cider—hard cider. But as the temperance movement of the mid-to-late 1800s gained momentum, teetotalers (those who marked pledge cards with a T, to signify total abstinence from alcohol) searched for alternate uses of apples. During this period, a profusion of dishes appeared, including homely-sounding pudding variants like apple grunts and apple slumps. Of course, apple pies proliferated.

■ Concurrent with the rise of the temperance movement came a drop in the price of grain and the mass migration of Germans to our shores. In time, the Germans made beer, which, for those still inclined toward alcoholic beverages, soon replaced cider as the preferred tipple. Faced with slews of cheap apples and

silos of cheap wheat flour, frugal cooks turned to—
what else?—pies.

▦ Apple trees flourished on American soil. In time,
the young nation came to be touted as a godly republic
boasting a munificent ecology. These were the days
when that folkloric haint, Johnny Appleseed, walked
about the Midwest, and Henry Ward Beecher, brother
of Harriet, opined that "of all fruits, no other can pretend to vie with the apple as the fruit of the common
people." These were the days when apple pie came to
be a symbol of said munificence.

▦ During the Civil War, both Union and Confederate
troops scavenged for apples and commandeered the
hearths—and flour bins—of white farmers and black
tenants to bake pies. Thusly wartime adversity fixed the
taste of apple pie on the palate of generations to come.
Numerous wartime diaries and letters support the hypothesis, including this 1863 entry from a soldier in
Tennessee: "When the army was not too far from the
base of supplies we could get some flour instead of
hard tack," he wrote. "Then the soldiers could go to
the negro cabins and dwelling houses and unceremo-
niously borrow or carry away these bake ovens. One
could bake anywhere with them, in the house or out of
doors, rain or sunshine, wherever hot embers could be
obtained. Soldiers could get green apples, slice them
into thin pieces, roll out crusts made from the flour, lay
in the sliced apples and cover with another crust."

■ Last, and perhaps most plausibly, as America co-opted the Industrial Revolution, apple pie came to be equated with an ascendant, even triumphant, affluence. "On the shoals of roast beef and apple pie," wrote a German economist, "all socialistic utopias founder." Four years earlier, in 1902, an Englishman hinted at a similar belief when he suggested, in a newspaper editorial, that a slice of apple pie per day was tantamount to gluttony. He believed two slices per week would do.

A *New York Times* editorial writer shot back: "It is utterly insufficient as anyone who knows the secret of our strength as a nation and the foundation of our industrial supremacy must admit. Pie is the American synonym for prosperity, and its varying contents the calendar of the changing seasons. PIE IS THE FOOD OF THE HEROIC. No pie-eating people can ever be vanquished."

i once believed that these stories of American apple pie demanded a pageant, one of those sweeping and histrionic outdoor dramas. At the time, I thought apple pie might be on the verge of irrelevancy, and that such a drama could inspire a renaissance or, at the very least, serve as a requiem. I imagined it as a musical, perhaps written by Tony Kushner. I foresaw it as a celebration and explication of our ongoing apple pie dialogue and diet. And then I learned that a young Brooklyn-based artist, Anissa Mack, had already staged such a pageant. Sort of.

during the summer of 2002, Anissa baked apple pies in a storybook cottage set in the shadow of the Brooklyn Public Library on a glorified median entangled by bus and car traffic. The diminutive house, built by Amish craftsmen, was finished with clapboard siding and a shingled roof. Red and white gingham curtains and powder-blue shutters framed window boxes planted with petunias. A hand-hewn spice rack decked the far wall. A tabletop oven hugged the back.

Four days a week during May and June, she worked at a pine table in the center of the cottage. Specks of flour usually dotted her freckled nose. She always dressed in an apron stitched by her own hand. Four times a day, she pulled a scratch apple pie from an oven and placed it on the windowsill to cool. And then she stood back to see what happened next. She called her participatory artwork *Pies for a Passerby*.

Anissa was not new to the role of provocateur, having made a splash in the art world a few years back when she crafted a pair of ruby slippers like the ones worn by Judy Garland in *The Wizard of Oz*. After depositing her replicas in front of a Smithsonian exhibit containing the originals, Anissa watched as museum patrons began trying on the slippers and, in time, taking pictures as souvenirs.

She applied a similarly populist ethic to apple pie. Informed by, among other cultural touchstones, the Norman Rockwell image of a Depression-era tramp racing across a field with a steaming apple pie in his hands and a snarling dog at his heels, Anissa believed that soon after placing each pie on the sill, someone would come along and steal it. But would people actually play the role American pop culture plotted for them?

She succeeded in engaging her audience. Adults cut pies to share with children and then joined the tussle over slices. Teenagers swooped in to wrench pies from the hands of babes. And then there were the chance effects, like the rumor that raced through the grade schools of Brooklyn alleging that the pies were actually baked by Oompa Loompa–like midgets who bedded down in the cottage each night.

Long after she packed up her apron and rolling pin, Anissa met me for a cup of coffee and a slice of pie. I quickly learned that our quests were kindred. "The idea was to test the icon, to see how it functions in the everyday world," she told me. "What meaning does apple pie have when it transcends the ideal and becomes corporeal? What does it mean when a real apple pie emerges from a real quaint little house?"

Anissa got her answers each time she pulled an apple pie from the oven and placed it on the windowsill. In time, she became—at least in the minds of passersby—a kind of oracle of apple pie. Mothers inquired about what brand of flour she preferred. Grandmothers admired the stitchwork on her apron. Farmers from the market across the way stopped by to talk of apples. Vegans talked of lard. Fathers picked up orders after work. Children camped out in front of the cottage door, fork in hand. And over the course of a long and hot summer, Anissa Mack proved that apple pie can be a catalyst for community development, that apple pie is a fulcrum for civic myth-making. In short, she proved that apple pie still matters.

the pages that follow catalogue my attempt to explore these ideas more deeply. Please know that I do not take myself seriously. But I do, when warranted, take my subject seriously. I intend this to be a portrait of America as seen through the lens of apple pie. And yes, I am aware that it can be difficult to *see* through pie, what with all those apples in the way. But I'll give it my all.

Apple Pie for a Passerby

Anissa, a Connecticut-born artist now living in Brooklyn, adapted the following recipe from Betty Crocker's Cookbook. *Over the course of a few dozen summer afternoons, she*

(continued)

perfected it while working in a de facto dollhouse outfitted with a toaster oven but no air-conditioning. Hers is a straightforward apple pie, an appropriately unfussy take on the national obsession.

CRUST

- ⅔ cup vegetable shortening, chilled
- ½ tablespoon salt
- 2 cups flour
- 4 to 5 tablespoons cold water

With a pastry cutter or a fork, cut the shortening and salt into the flour until the mix is pebbly. Add the water and stir with a fork until the dough becomes somewhat sticky. Form dough into a ball, and then cut the ball in half, handling the dough as little as possible. Wrap in plastic and refrigerate, preferably for at least an hour.

FILLING

- 5 cups chopped apples, preferably McIntosh
- ⅓ cup white sugar
- ¼ cup brown sugar
- ½ teaspoon cinnamon
- ¼ teaspoon nutmeg
- ½ tablespoon salt
- 2 tablespoons uncooked tapioca (to thicken)

Mix all the ingredients in a deep bowl. Stir well to combine.

FINISH

Roll the dough out into two circles that are 3 inches in diameter wider than your pie shell or plate. Line the pie plate with the first dough and spoon in the filling. Lay the second dough atop, and crimp the edges together. Pierce the top crust 6 or 8 times with a sharp knife so that steam will be released. Cook at 425°F for 50–60 minutes or until you see sugar bubbling out of the cuts in the crust.

Here's Pie in Your Eye

my conversation with Anissa gets me thinking about other intersections of art and pie. And that gets me to pondering the point where mannerly gouache meets velvet Elvis, where opera buffa meets the Three Stooges. Instead of employing my traditional mode of investigation—ensconcing myself in the library or jetting away on a pie-eating excursion—I settle in to watch Larry fling pies at Curly and Moe. More than two weeks pass before I set out for the epicenter of commercial apple growing, Washington state, and during that time I become as serious a student of the pie toss as that peculiar art will allow.

I discover the existence of the films *Pies and Guys* and *In the Sweet Pie and Pie,* but I am not able to lay hands on copies. Yet after working my way through a number of other Three Stooges films, I am able to identify classic flings including the discus toss and the pitcher-catcher toss. Still, though I must have witnessed a couple hundred tosses, I have not have seen the flight of a single *apple* pie.

It seems that meringue-capped cream pies have long been preferred for on-screen flings, beginning with the first documented toss in the 1913 film *A Noise from the Deep* and continuing through the Laurel and Hardy short, *Battle of the Century.* (The latter, at 3,000 pies, required the entire daily output of the Los Angeles Pie Company.) Alas, there remains scant evidence of apple-pie tossing. Evidently faux pies of nothing but meringue were less likely to cause a concussion and promised better visuals.

ONE

Fruit Stand
Death March

three slices into a seven-slice day, I'm casting about for a phrase that encapsulates my explorations in Washington state. "Pie Marches On" is too cute. Besides, pie king Monroe Strause wrote a book by that title years ago. "Fruit Stand Death March," on the other hand, evokes the spirit of the quest, the possible travails of the single-minded pursuit of great apple pie.

At my side is Seattle attorney and inveterate gourmand Peter McKee, who understands the import of my mission and has volunteered to drive his minivan to the ends of the earth—or at least the Idaho border. Thanks to contacts made by Peter, I had the opportunity to meet with a labor organizer who might, in turn, introduce me to Mexican migrants who work the apple orchards and make pies from wormed fruit. And I had a standing invitation from the mayor of Wenatchee, who promised hard-hat tours of apple-storage warehouses and apple-juicing plants as well as an audience with the band of bakers who, in 1997, created what the *Guinness Book of World Records* then recognized as the world's largest apple pie.

Though such research has guided me in other investigations, this time my gut tells me to try another tack. This time, my operating theory is this: Washington is the epicenter of American apple production, where growers harvest more than fifteen billion apples each year. So a search for totemic apple pie should require no more forethought than showing up hungry, at harvest time, where the roadside is thick with groves, the trees burdened by yellow and red orbs.

I n the beginning, our meandering did not show great promise. The first two pies we sampled while driving west, up and over the mighty Cascade range, made a mockery of their heritage. We dubbed the first slice to be a "slag heap of corn syrup and canned fruit." Peter, a bespectacled man of slight build and great humor, damned the second as "befouled by the chemical tang of freezer burn." Unlike Peter, I was inclined to forgive the freezer-burn pie, for it was the product of a café that caters to truckers hauling frozen foods to the port of Seattle. Those fellows might actually *like* the taste of Freon.

Slice three is the first that approaches my ideal, and the first that can claim linkage to the fruit stands we hope will function as lodestars. Set at the base of the fir-rimmed valley cut by Peshatin Creek, the low-slung Big-Y Café is recommended by the folks at Nicholson Orchards, who sell a variety of heirloom apples from their roadside lean-to, including a mottled-red-and-yellow variety known as Swiss Gourmet. Just ask for Helen, they said, she'll fix you up.

Helen Rayfield does not disappoint. Known to her friends as Blab, known to her admirers as the Royal Lady of the Autumn Leaves (a title bestowed on her in a 1994 coronation at the nearby Best Western Icicle Inn), she is a sixty-something-year-old student of the apple industry who prefers local Jonagolds for her pies and knows a good baker when she hires one.

After breaking through a firm top crust dusted with sugar and digging my fork into a stratum of apples that shines purple with cinnamon, I tell Helen how much I like the pie. She looks me up and down. "We got a little girl in the back by the name of Stacy," she says. "You can see for yourself that she's a great baker, and you know what? She's not married, not even engaged!" Though I politely decline Helen's proffer of romance, I ask Stacy's last name in an effort to document the first Washington woman to win my palate. "I don't know, honey," Helen says with a snort that morphs into a chuckle. "I just hired her and haven't even written her name on a paycheck. You can call her Stacy Baker."

Our next fruit-stand tip comes while cruising the aisles of Prey's Fruit Barn, an outsized emporium of apples and pears and all manner of tchotchkes. When I ask an employee whether they sell apple pies, she tells me that Home Fires Bakery, nearby in the faux-Bavarian village of Leavenworth, is the place we seek. "They buy our Jonagolds," she says, by way of endorsement.

We thread our way past a timber-embellished RadioShack and a gingerbread-trimmed Dairy Queen that could be the Friday-night hang of Hansel and Gretel. Though I am dubious that any honest apple pie could be cooked amongst such dishonest surroundings, I bound onto the tin-roofed porch of Home Fires Bakery and through the screened door. Visions of sugarplums—and apple pies—dance in my head.

The crumb-topped pie, served in a small tin, is rather good. The real problem is my own, for I cannot shake the knowledge that this little town is no more Bavarian than Boise, Idaho. Like a number of places faced with the departure of industry and the demise of rail service, Leavenworth reimagined its business district in the 1970s, recasting the village as a tourist attraction where all the lederhosen-clad men play in oompah bands, and all the women wear plaid jumpers while sloshing tankards of ale from tap to table. Somehow, when I bite into the Home Fires apple pie, I taste that troweled shellac, that Bavarian artifice.

Peter and I press on. If you're keeping score, we're batting .250. And I'm growing a tad grumpy. I mutter, half to myself, half to Peter: Is it too much to ask that I eat an honest apple pie at an honest-to-God fruit stand? Though Peter is wont to concur, he can't help but grow a tad defensive when I inveigh against his home state.

Maybe it's desperation. Maybe it's pie-drunk hubris. But before I know it, Peter has turned into the parking lot of a candy factory in the burg of Cashmere. I believe I can guess why. A few hours earlier, I'd told him of an upcoming trip to Iowa where I planned to visit an apple grower who has staked her pie reputation on the addition of cinnamon Red Hots candies to her filling. If I read my friend's instincts right, he's thinking that Aplets—the apple-flavored candies made here, the ones advertised as the "Confection of the Faeries"— might make a grand addition to an apple pie.

My mind reels. Perhaps the Aplets people are already marketing such a concoction. Perhaps their head candy chemist will be on hand to greet us and offer consultation on how to combine Aplets and apples. The cash-register clerk, however, will have none of this. "They tried that one year at our pie contest," she tells me. "But the pectin and corn syrup in

the candy just turned to goo and the pie turned all chewy."
Peter grimaces. And I make a mental note to call my source
in Iowa and inquire about the "goo factor" before I book a
flight.

back on the road, the sun wanes as we round a bend.
The Columbia River thrums by on our right. Craggy
cliffs pocked with gnarled scrub rise on our left beyond the
macadam. The last two hours have not been productive. After
the Aplets misadventure, we stopped at three more fruit
stands. Not one served apple pie.

When we abandoned the fruit-stand ideal and snagged a
booth at Prospector Pies in Wenatchee, Peter took one bite of
pie and declared it to be "a factory excretion." At least he was
kind enough to say it sotto voce. I, on the other hand, told
our teenage server what I thought of her pie. And no, upon
reflection, even the five-dollar tip I slipped under my coffee
cup didn't make up for my indiscretion.

I asked a clerk at the Sunshine Fruit Market near Lake
Chelan why we were having so much trouble finding fruit
stands that serve apple pie. "Maybe apple growers have grown
too lazy," she said. "Maybe apples are too much with us." As
Peter drives on, past groves of green tucked into mountain-
sides, I think about her observation, about my expectations,
and about how far we are from Seattle. Peter argues for one
more stop, one more chance. It's close to six in the evening,
and we've been on the road since seven in the morning. As it

is, our return trip will take four hours, but we both know we owe ourselves one last slice. Peter chooses the destination: Lone Pine Fruit and Espresso.

Again, I begin to wonder aloud again about whether the apparent disconnect between farm and table hereabouts has something to do with the industrial model on which the Washington apple industry is based. Though there has been a recent spike of interest in heirloom apples, Washington is still best known as the home of the Red Delicious, a hardy variety that can be long on looks and short on flavor. In converting to the large-scale cultivation of apples as commodity, have Washington growers distanced themselves from the kitchen? Perhaps—John Thorne's assertion to the contrary—cold storage and long-haul trucking mean that it no longer matters where your apples are grown.

Fortunately for Peter, such pondering ceases when, just as the sun fades behind the fir, the Lone Pine comes into view. Set amidst a bleak landscape of basalt hoodoos, the building looks like a cowboy bunkhouse of late-nineteenth-century vintage, albeit one that advertises espresso. According to a brochure we picked up along the way, they are set to close in ten minutes, so I clamber up the steps with Peter following close behind.

Just inside the door is a pastry case, empty except for an apple pie with two or three slices remaining. When I ask the woman behind the counter if they grew the fruit that fills the tin, she points toward the rear of the store where bins of apples line the wall. "This pie's got some Gala for crunch, and some Jonagold for bite," she says. "Of course they're our apples—why would we use somebody else's?" Between forkfuls, I turn my attention to learning the name of the baker. The counterwoman is not forthcoming. Rather than push the issue, I seize the opportunity to reimagine our lodestar, and dub the mystery woman Tracy Baker—sister of Stacy.

Lone Pine Pie

This is an exercise in subtlety. Once rendered into pie, can you distinguish one variety of apple from another from another? Does the interplay of textures and flavors dance on your tongue or are the Galas and Jonagolds swamped by the cinnamon and vanilla? Me, I'm a goner for this pie, and for the kiss of cider in the crust. One taste goes a long way toward buoying my opinion of Washington state.

CRUST

- 1 egg, separated
- ½ tablespoon cider vinegar
- ¾ cup warm water
- 3 cups all-purpose flour

- 1 cup lard (or shortening)
- 1½ teaspoons salt

In a liquid measuring cup, stir egg yolk with cider vinegar and enough warm water to reach the ½-cup mark. Set aside. Put flour, lard, and salt into a mixing bowl. Combine. Add egg mixture, stir, and form two balls. Place one between two sheets of plastic wrap and with a rolling pin press into a disk large enough to overlap the edges of your pie plate. Repeat with second dough ball. Refrigerate doughs for at least an hour.

FILLING

- 2 large spicy apples, Galas if you can find them
- 3 large sweet apples, Jonagolds if you can find them
- juice of ½ lemon
- ½ cup dark brown sugar
- 1 tablespoon all-purpose flour
- 1 teaspoon cinnamon
- 1 teaspoon vanilla
- ½ teaspoon salt
- ¼ teaspoon freshly ground nutmeg
- 1½ tablespoons butter

(continued)

Peel and slice apples. In a bowl, mix apples, lemon juice, dark brown sugar, flour, cinnamon, vanilla, salt, and nutmeg with your hands. Set aside.

FINISH

Heat the oven to 375°F. Roll the dough into two circles that are 2–3 inches wider in diameter than your pie shell or plate. Place one crust in the pie plate. Pour filling atop the crust and dot with nubbins of butter. Cut a central vent in the top crust. Place top crust over the filling and crimp the edges. Glaze the top crust with egg white mixed with 1 tablespoon of water. Sprinkle with sugar. Bake at 375°F for 15 minutes. Reduce heat to 350°F and bake for another 45 minutes or so.

Pop-Up Iowa

i had high hopes for Iowa. I figured that, amidst amber waves of grain, beneath a cobalt sky, I would come to know Middle America and come to eat middlebrow apple pie. That's middlebrow as in nothing too fancy, nothing too chancy. After my Washington sojourn, I took comfort in the promise of straight-arrow Iowa. Yet, as would prove to be the case many times during my explorations, I was deluded.

Emily Martin, an Iowa City maker of art books, set me straight. I knew of her work before I hit the road, knew that in her basement studio she crafted one-of-a-kind Iowa pop-up books from which sprang wire tornados and origami corn stalks. But what I did not fully appreciate was her dedication to pastry as art: Taking apple pie as her inspiration, she has crafted a series of *pies,* each comprised of slice-shaped books, each slice embossed with a lattice crust, a homily, and a recipe.

Emily proves a boon. I visit her studio and purchase a full set of pie books for my burgeoning apple-pie-as-icon collection. And at Emily's insistence, I pledge to visit her favorite local haunt, Hamburg Inn #2. According to Emily, it's home to another Iowa innovation: the apple-pie shake.

TWO

Blinded by Irony

emily Martin was not the first person to tell me of the fabled apple-pie shakes of Iowa City, Iowa. The first was my friend Matt Lee, who, with his brother, Ted, runs the Lee Brothers Boiled Peanut Company. While writing this very chapter, I found an old note to self: "Matt says pie shakes are the thing at the Hamburg Inn, Iowa City." I came upon that forgotten note long after I returned home from my Iowa travels, where, luckily, others had steered me in the same direction. Never mind that you might expect a fellow writing a book on apple pie to remember such a tip without aid of note or mnemonic.

Phoebe Lawless of Magnolia Grill in Durham, North Carolina, made a deeper impression. Chalk it up to the fact that she makes a mean peanut butter and bacon truffle, has cartoon salt and pepper shakers tattooed on her left bicep, and hosts an annual pie party during which she and her husband and their friends engage in orgiastic appreciation of the dish. In any case, I was paying closer attention when *she* told me of the pie shakes proffered by a certain Iowa City diner.

Yet even with the endorsement of the lovely and talented Phoebe, I remained suspect of the entire pie-shake genre. It took Emily's entreaty to seal the deal. Even then, I postponed visiting the Hamburg Inn until after I went gallivanting halfway across the state in search of a woman known for showering her apple-pie filling with cinnamon Red Hots.

i do not regret the gallivanting. Driving north and west out of Iowa City and into the countryside beyond the farm town of Jefferson, I glimpse a gilded Iowa through blond corn tassels that sway at eye level. I hear Iowa by way of radio advertisements for Monday-night ice cream socials, Wednesday-night prayer meetings, Friday-night football games. And at the kitchen table of farmwoman Cindy Deal, I taste Iowa, digging my fork deep into a generous slice of pie, stacked high with her family's Lodis and Jonathans.

Standing at her kitchen counter, a shower of crumbs at my

feet, I admire how the Red Hots melt into the apples and stain the crust vents a lovely shade of coral. Cindy, a middle-aged woman straight out of midwestern central casting, smiles. I marvel at her ability to roll a crust of unerring tenderness and flakiness. But she demurs any authorship of recipe or technique. She perceives no alchemy at work. She points only to the quality of the apples grown on their farm by her husband, Gerald.

"The crust is one I took from Betty Crocker and changed some," she says. "And the Red Hots are nothing new. That's something that's been around for a while now. I always heard that one of Gerald's brothers challenged their mother to bake a different pie every day for a month. Maybe it came from there, but it could have just as easily been some woman from a long time ago who was out of cinnamon."

As I listen to Cindy, I survey her kitchen: Draped over a chair is a freshly darned softball uniform. On a yellow linoleum counter sit a tub of Crisco and a five-pound sack of flour. Out in the yard, a dog barks. I am in the bosom of Middle America, in the presence of an unfalteringly modest woman who bakes immodest apple pies. She's telling me that she owes it all to her family and Betty Crocker. And yet I cannot resist the urge to establish a kind of ironic distance from my subject.

Perhaps it's the curse of my generation: always resisting naked earnestness, ever in search of the conceits at the core of human interaction. Prior to our kitchen tête-à-tête, I had unconsciously assigned Cindy's Red Hot apple pie to the same category of confections as the deep-fried Twinkie-on-a-stick. I thought she was in on the joke. But there was no punch line lurking beneath her crust. Cindy Deal does not sully her filling with ironic filigree. For that effect, I'll have to head elsewhere.

So I press on. Could irony explain the other Iowa riff on apple pie, the pie shake? I succumb to the suggestions of my friends and head for Iowa City and the Hamburg Inn. College towns, if I recall correctly, are hotbeds of irony.

The Hamburg Inn appears to be a schlumpy diner, the kind of plywood-paneled gathering place where grad students stoked on coffee and Kant share the counter with sheetrock hangers and beat cops and bovine veterinarians. Despite the fact that my sources tell me apple-pie shakes were invented—or at least popularized—here, no one is partaking of this peculiar delicacy when I stride through the door.

I arrive, full of myself, full of questions: *Is the pie shake an example of the Iowa flair for frugality? Or is it a trumped-up dessert of recent vintage and ironic artifice?* When the evidence begins to mount in favor of the former theory, I wonder, *What is the pie shake but a milk shake into which has been pulsed a ruined slice, a day-old wedge with a busted crust?*

With these thoughts ricocheting about, I swivel onto a stool and snag a menu. Though the apple-pie shake is to be my locus of investigation, the Hamburg Inn serves all manner of pies and mixes all manner of pie shakes, including blueberry, pumpkin, cherry, peach, lemon, and rhubarb.

In due time, my shake arrives in a frost-skirted blender cup. It's a beautiful sight to behold, and even better to taste: Chock-full of crust fragments and crushed apple slices, the shake calls to mind a better class of Dairy Queen Blizzard. At about the same time the shake arrives, so does Hamburg Inn majordomo Steve Fugate. He's no grad student—but he is a twenty-three-year veteran of the Hamburg Inn, with a philosophical bent.

Over the course of a rambling conversation, I discover that he's predisposed to philosophical musings about everything from organic gardening to griddled versus charcoal-grilled burgers. But he's not one to conjure an elaborate creation story when a simple one will do. The story of the pie shake, as told by Fugate, the frugal diner operator, is a what-you-see-is-what-you-get scenario.

I consider asking Fugate about the possibility of designing my own apple-pie shake, of slipping a leftover slice from one of Cindy Deal's Red Hot homemade apple pies in his blender cup. But since her pie is in perfect shape, such an act would violate the Iowa ethic of frugality. Instead I decide to wait until I return home, where I can take matters (and pie) into my own hands.

two nights later, spent from a day of canceled flights and missed connections, I stumble into my kitchen, pie box in hand. My wife and son are asleep. I reach beneath the sink for our blender. I shovel in pie from the box Cindy Deal gave me, taking care to get sufficient crust into the vessel. I add two mounds of ice cream and some milk.

When I hit the toggle switch, the shake froths white, turns beige as the crust and apples emulsify, and then, finally, blushes the barest shade of pink as the Red Hots combust. I take a sip, noting the hint of cinnamon, the pleasantly chunky texture. Irony or ingenuity? Hell if I know, but I'm betting pink is a flattering color for a milkshake mustache.

Cindy Deal's Red Hot Apple Pie

It's important to space the Red Hots well, for they are not ironic; they are the sole source of cinnamon in this pie. If the gods smile upon your pie, the Red Hots within will retain some of their structure, will still snap and send a little jolt of heat when you bite down. Since meeting Cindy Deal, I've come across numerous references to this pie. The earliest was in a 1949 pamphlet, Aunt Chick's Pies, *marketed by Nettie McBirney of Tulsa, Oklahoma. Aunt Chick suggests a lattice crust and instructs that once the pie is halfway done, the cook drop candies in "every open square of the lattice."*

CRUST

- Use one of the recipes from pages 10, 20, 39, or 78.

FILLING

- 5 tart apples, peeled, cored, and sliced
(Lodis or Jonathans are ideal.)
- ¾ cup sugar
- 2 tablespoons flour
- dash of salt
- ¼ cup honey
- 2 dozen or so Red Hots, known generically
as cinnamon imperials
- 2 tablespoons butter
- 1 egg, beaten

Heat oven to 400°F. Combine ½ cup sugar with the flour and salt. Set aside.

Roll the dough into two circles that are 2–3 inches wider in diameter than your pie shell or plate. Line the pie pan or plate with the bottom crust. Fill halfway with apples. Drizzle on half of the honey. Sprinkle on half of the sugar mixture. Mound the remaining apples, and then drizzle on the remainder of the honey and sprinkle on the remainder of the sugar mixture.

(continued)

Space the Red Hots evenly throughout the filling.
Cut the butter into bits and dot the entire filling with
them. Cut slits in the top crust and place it over the filling, crimping the edges as you go. Paint the egg on the
crust and sprinkle with the remaining sugar. Bake at
400°F for 15 minutes and then reduce the temperature to 350°F and bake for 45 minutes or until brown.

Apple Pie Shake
à la mode de la Hamburg Inn

- 1 cup of milk
- 2 scoops vanilla ice cream
- small slice of pie

Combine ingredients in a blender and pulse until just
shy of a puree. Texture is all-important here, so go easy
on the toggle switch.

How Long Is Your Flake?

onroe Boston Strause, the self-proclaimed Pie King of America during the 1930s and 1940s, delineated three types of piecrust: short flake, medium flake, and long flake. As flake length increases, said Strause, crusts become tougher.

The best apple-pie crusts are liminal. They exhibit a shortness that translates into tenderness, while at the same time boasting sufficient integrity—and flake length—that the crust does not crumble into a heap.

Like much having to do with pie, the concept of flake is misunderstood. Oftentimes we toss about terms like shortbread—as in strawberry shortcake—when we don't know what in the hell we're talking about. (Shortbreads, by the way, have exceptionally short—or tender—crusts, and crumble easily.) Until I spent an afternoon baking with Karen Barker, whose story follows, I had given little thought to how flake length affects the tender-to-sturdy piecrust continuum, preferring instead to believe the making of a perfect crust to be an act of legerdemain.

Since, I've learned flake is simple: it merely refers to what happens when fats coat the strands of gluten in wheat flour— they literally shorten them. Yet all fats do not shorten with the same efficacy. And this, of course, plays into the eternal butter-versus-lard piecrust debate. Here's the skinny on the fats:

Butter, because it usually contains 80 percent fat and 20 percent water, shortens (or tenderizes) less effectively than does lard, which is 100 percent fat. But butter carries flavor. So many a cook stirs butter and lard together to reach the tender-tasty ideal.

THREE

Mystery of the Frigid Digits

along with her husband, Ben, Karen Barker owns Magnolia Grill, a storefront restaurant in Durham, North Carolina, that has won a nationwide reputation for tweaking the American canon with dishes like sage-and-bourbon-marinated quail on crawfish risotto, and gingerbread waffles with cardamom ice cream. Named America's best pastry chef for 2003 by the James Beard Foundation, Karen is a slight woman with curly black hair and quick brown eyes. She's also generous—when I pick up the phone and ask her to tutor me in the art of crust, she does not blanch; she just asks when I want to make the trek to her home.

What you really need to know about Karen is that she has cold hands—so cold it's as if her heart pumps soft-serve ice cream through her veins. We are standing in her suburban kitchen when I learn this. Given her belief that a great piecrust requires the chilling of everything from the water that binds the dough to the bowl in which the dough is mixed, such an accident of anatomy might be understood as an omen of pastry predestination.

Karen doesn't dismiss the possibility that some great pie makers are born with a kind of tactile supremacy, that they are uniquely equipped to work fat into flour in the pursuit of the perfect piecrust. But to her credit, she's the kind of person who doesn't warm to terms like pastry predestination.

Karen is a pragmatist—a pragmatist who clamps her icy hand on my forearm to illustrate the proper temperature at which it's safe to combine flour and fat without the heat from said hands melting the fat and losing the flakiness that defines a superior crust. A pragmatist who doesn't even trust her cold hands to do the job, relying instead upon pulsing the flour and fat in the chilled bowl of a food processor.

This emphasis upon detail is a revelation. Before sitting down at Karen's kitchen counter, I thought the attention to detail employed by the best bakers was superfluous. I gauged it to be somehow fussy, in the same way a six-year-old boy appraises an eight-year-old girl's tea set. Until now, I had merely an architectural appreciation for a firm and yet flaky crust.

But over the course of an afternoon under Karen's tutelage I come to believe that crust is all. I now know that a frugal mixture of flour and fat and water is the backbone upon which all great pies are built. Sure, it's important to strike a sublime balance between sweet and tart when mixing apples and sugar and spices, but, according to my new worldview, without an honest crust you're doomed to fall short of the platonic pie ideal.

Karen's instruction for piecrust is detailed at the end of this chapter, and it's a great recipe. But even the best recipes can't convey what it's like to be in the presence of a baker like Karen. The beauty, the truth, is in the details. After she cuts frozen butter and shortening into her flour, the result is not pea-sized clumps, though that's what many recipes call for. According to Karen, it should look like clumpy sand. And she's right, but I never would have known the difference had I not had the chance to lean in close. I fear that despite my best efforts you may never get it right, that there's no written substitute for leaning over her shoulder.

After Karen spritzes water into her clumpy sand, she gathers the dough up into a ball. It feels like Play-Doh—I pinch off a piece and instantly recall that texture of childhood. Later, when the dough emerges from an hour or two in the refrigerator, it appears marbleized. Ghost clumps of butter hover in suspension behind a veil of emulsified dough. I trace my fingers along the pattern, admiring the silkiness of the emulsified dough and the delicacy of the veiled butter nubs. And yet I daresay that Karen's recipe for piecrust fails to convey this look and feel, and I know full well that my prose will never match the sensation.

Like other tactile truths revealed by Karen, words will surely fail to convey what it is like to watch Karen attack a crust. She wields a rolling pin with authority, and she eschews the use of what she calls "little ol' Barbie pins." Karen's model is crafted from maple and recalls, in girth and weight, the trunk from which it was hewn. She does not roll it across the dough until she has formed a crust of sufficient circumference to fit a pie plate. No, Karen beats that dough, cocking her body like a spring-loaded jackhammer, slamming the pin down with such force that the ball bearings within chime and the table beneath the crust shudders.

Truth be told, to appreciate Karen's way with a pie, you need to try it yourself. On a Friday afternoon not long after I return home, I take my own advice, picking up a rolling pin and setting to work on a crust. On my mind is a phone call I received earlier in the day, from a gentleman lawyer and avid eater who lives near the Barkers. As an aside to our conversation about the manly enterprise of barbecue, I note that he must be proud that the James Beard Foundation named Karen, a fellow North Carolinian, the best pastry chef in America.

But the attorney-cum-gourmand surprises me. After offering perfunctory praise for her way with a pie, he says, "You know, she's really not a pastry chef. She's more of a baker."

When I profess to be unaware of the distinction, he tells me that a pastry chef is more of a high-wire act. A pastry chef takes chances. What Karen does is not dramatic or inventive enough to be called pastry work.

At first I shrug off his comments as typical of a lawyer bent on parsing all manner of human endeavor. But midway through his soliloquy on Brunswick stew, I connect the dots back to my onetime myopia. Fueled by chauvinistic guilt, I lay into him. I get nowhere. So I call Karen and tattle on him. I don't actually tell her who he is, but I do share his comments. I'm hoping she'll wield a rolling pin in defense of her title. But Karen just sighs. "If a pastry chef wants to build a spun-sugar cage around a slice of apple pie, that's fine by me," she says. "Besides, baker sounds forthright and honest. I like that."

Karen Barker's
Pin-Rattling Piecrust

More than perhaps any crust recipe in this book, Karen's requires dexterity and experience. But give it your all and this crust pays big dividends in taste and flake. Try it a couple of

(continued)

times and judge for yourself. And if you still don't think your
pie measures up to the standard set by Karen, I suggest you
make a pilgrimage to Magnolia Grill, where, in addition to
regular ol' apple and rhubarb-apple pies, Karen and Phoebe
roll out lemon Shaker pies, mocha-molasses shoofly pies, maple-
bourbon sweet-potato pies, and key-lime coconut pies.

- 2⅔ cups all-purpose flour
- ¾ teaspoon kosher salt
- ¾ tablespoon sugar
- 4 ounces butter, chilled and cut into pieces
- 4 ounces vegetable shortening, chilled and cut into pieces
- ¼ to ½ cup water, chilled in a squeeze bottle or spray bottle

Pulse flour, salt, and sugar in a food processor until blended. Add butter and shortening and pulse 12 to 14 times or until the mixture looks like clumpy sand. Transfer mixture to a large bowl and gradually spray in enough cold water to form a cohesive and evenly moistened dough that is still not sticky. Work quickly, tossing and stirring with a fork until dough begins to come together. Divide dough in two. Shape each half into a flattened round. Wrap in plastic and chill in the refrigerator for several hours or overnight. To prepare dough for the pie plate, lay down a sheet of wax paper. With a rolling pin, bang out the rounds into crusts, making initial impact at the centermost point before stroking quickly outward. Lift the pin each time before whacking it again. Ten or twelve spankings should do it. This crust recipe works well with just about any filling.

Bag It!

Karen Barker is a student of the old ways. Buy quality ingredients. Lavish attention upon your crust. And bake fifty or sixty pies. Eventually, you'll get the hang of it.

But there are many bakers who rely upon a gimmick, and the most widespread gimmick is to bake a pie in a paper bag. It seems to be a particular favorite of midwestern bakers. The Elegant Farmer in Mukwonago, Wisconsin, stakes its reputation on a paper-bag pouch. Ditto the Dutch Harvest Restaurant, an Amish enterprise in Berlin, Ohio.

After eating a few paper-bag apple pies and talking to three or four bakers who swear by the practice, I still remain unclear of the benefits: Does the paper bag do nothing more than ensure that the apple-pie goo doesn't splatter onto oven walls? Or does something magical happen between those brown pulp sheets?

When I ask the bakers what happens and why, they imply that while the pie is in the bag and out of sight, unseen forces wreak unknown influence. In the end, I conclude that magic is the promise of every pie. And a top crust of the kind Karen rolls out provides sufficient cover for transformations of both gastronomical and metaphysical sorts.

FOUR

Tootie Feagan's
Four-Pound Pie

i n the early days of our republic, the makings of a pie were called timber. As in, "Do
you have enough timber for a pie?" Implicit
was the acknowledgment that a sturdy crust
filled with honest apples is a thing of substance,
best described in terms used by craftsmen.
When William Maginn, a nineteenth-century
chronicler of the drinking class, asked, "What
is a roofless cathedral to a well-built pie?" he
hinted at a similar belief: that apple pies merit

aesthetic appraisal rooted in both architectural and gastronomic impulses.

While researching this book, I spent weeks on end wandering about in pursuit of iconic apple pies, but I probably
spent an equal amount of time among the stacks in various li-
braries, tracing the evolution of pies and pie bakers. One day,
while scrolling through a reel of microfilm, I learned that the
historical intertwining of architecture and pie long preceded
our nation's founding.

Pies of yore were utilitarian products, I read. Crusts were
built to be standing vessels with structural integrity. Their
purpose was not to convey flavor, but to serve as containers.
(One of the early terms for crust was "coffyn," sharing a heritage with "coffin"; during Roman times, savory pie fillings
were stored in inedible structures called reeds.) The paradig-
matic tender and flaky crust, it seems, is a rather recent
development.

Perhaps this historical impulse to build an architec-
turally sound confection with walls of the kind a levee
engineer might imagine is antecedent to a more recent trend
toward gargantuan pies. Throughout the country—at Reading Terminal Market in Philadelphia, at the Auburn Avenue
Curb Market in Atlanta—bakers are engineering manhole-
sized heel crusts, heaped with five or more pounds of sliced
apples, the whole secreted beneath circus tents of top crust.

My first instinct was to condemn the elephantine pie phe-

nomenon as a reflection of the fast-food tendency toward su-
persizing any and all consumables. But after listening to my
crust-as-construction-project rumination, my wife, Blair, came
up with another theory.

Her belief is that some people can't stop washing their
hands. Others dull their scissors clipping grocery coupons
they never plan to use. And others still are obsessive builders,
intent upon raising an edifice of sufficient grandeur to satisfy
a slightly skewed internal barometer.

Blair sees the latter impulse in a home near ours in
Oxford, Mississippi. The brick colonial, fronted with Doric
columns, is rather formal for our neighborhood, but the real
disconnect comes when you notice what appears to be a
gymnasium tacked to the back end of the house. For what
seems like the past decade, our neighbor's McManse has
been under constant construction, metastasizing across prop-
erty lines as square footage doubles and triples, and stucco
façade begets stucco façade. Blair explains the ongoing development as the work of a woman with a building disorder.
After a few months of eating some very large pies, I am inclined to believe that the same pathology may animate many
a big pie.

tootie Feagan, founder of Tootie Pie in Medina, Texas, is
the acknowledged queen of the supersized apple pie.
She is also everyone's idea of a Rockwellian grandmother.
Her black-and-white hair is spun into a cotton-candy bun.

Her eyeglasses resemble butterflies frozen in mid-flight. Her smile is kind. Upon meeting the septuagenarian, I dismiss any possibility of pathology and devise a third theory of supersized pies. More on that in a minute.

Though she's now a master at rolling out crusts big enough to accommodate a bushel, Feagan was not born with a rolling pin in her grip. She was a tomboy who came late to the kitchen. "My mother died when I was thirteen," she tells me when I've pulled up a chair in the oversized tool shed that now serves as the headquarters for Tootie Pie. "So my daddy taught me to do it all. I rode horses bareback, could bulldog a calf in a dress. One time I broke our milk cow so that I could ride her. Daddy was pretty mad about that, because from that point on she wouldn't give any more milk."

Feagan didn't try her hand at pie until the 1970s. By that time, she had her own children. Her daughter responded by digging the apples out with a spoon and tossing the crust in a wastebasket. "I was a cake woman back then," she tells me. "My piecrusts were tough as whitleather—they would split when you cooked them. It took a while before I learned a better way."

an aside: I have made every effort to avoid sentimentality of the knee-jerk sort usually employed when apple pie is in play, so it is with no small measure of trepidation that I reveal the impetus for Tootie Feagan's education in the way of pie.

———

not long after my first husband passed away, I took a job with a hunting lodge," Feagan tells me, fast-forwarding to a time soon after her fifty-fifth birthday. "I cooked their meals and tended to them. That turned my life around: somebody needed me. I realized right then that I needed them, I needed to care for people." In the hill country beyond Medina, on a ranch where oilmen hunted deer and boar, Feagan says, she found her calling in the kitchen.

"In a way my community taught me to bake," she says, as I heft a buxom slice to my mouth and chomp down through a rich crust that does not so much shatter as flake apart. "But it just took me a while to pay attention. It was always with me; I always knew that when the farmers went from ranch to ranch, working together to cut and bale hay, the wives would work inside, shucking and boiling corn, frying chicken, baking pies. But I had never given enough thought to that. You know what I mean?"

Feagan continues: "I've been thinking about pie a little since then. I figure apple pie got to be popular because of apples. Long time ago, back before fresh apples were always in the store, you could slice apples up and dry them and save them for a winter pie. They kept good. Now that was back before the apple industry here really took off."

Feagan refers to the late-1980s boom in apple production that came with the planting of orchards amongst the scrubland northwest of San Antonio. At one time, apples were thought to be the ascendant crop hereabouts. I wonder aloud as to whether the boom could have been a catalyst for Feagan's construction of apple pies that weigh in at three, sometimes four or more pounds.

And soon, with Feagan taking the lead and me prodding here and there, we devise a theory that may well explain her big pies. Perhaps her tendency to heap the slices high has its origin in the days when, faced with a bumper crop supply of local apples—and remembering the days when they were a fruit to be hoarded—she celebrated the largesse of the local orchards by coring and slicing one more apple. And then another. And another.

Only problem is, Feagan tells me, apple production has since dropped and prices have escalated. "We use Washington state ones now," she says. "Golden Delicious, with some Braeburns too, if I can get them. And I can't often get them." As to why she continues to heap them high, Tootie says it might have something to do with being a Texan.

Though the "Texas grows 'em big" rationalization may seem facile, I can't deny that possibility. Not when I exit her pie hut and fix my eyes on the empty vista that rolls toward the horizon. After all, this is the kind of a state where grandiose notions take hold, I tell myself, where folks bury Cadillacs in the dirt and call the resulting structure a fence.

Pecan Apple Rye Pie

Mere mortals like me are not talented enough to turn out a four-pound pie. So I cast about for an alternative. I find inspiration in the pecan pie recipe from The Gift of Southern Cooking *by Edna Lewis and Scott Peacock. Pecan pie strikes me as an appropriate ode to Texas, for while the trees grow as far north as Iowa, and as far east as North Carolina, most botanists agree that the heart of the native growing region is Texas. You should also know that while Lewis and Peacock spike their pie with bourbon, I substitute rye whiskey. And, of course, I add a few apples.*

CRUST

Use one of the recipes on pages 10, 20, or 39. You need only one crust for this recipe, so you'll end up with a second for later use.

FILLING

- 2 apples, sliced and chopped
- 1 cup apple juice
- 3 eggs, lightly beaten
- 1 cup granulated sugar

(continued)

- ¼ cup light corn syrup
- ½ cup dark corn syrup
- ⅓ cup unsalted butter, melted
- 2 tablespoons rye whiskey (or bourbon or Tennessee whiskey)
- 1 teaspoon vanilla extract
- ¼ teaspoon salt
- ½ heaping cup coarsely chopped pecans

Cook apples in a saucepan with apple juice until they soften, about 10 minutes. Drain apples in a colander. Mix together the eggs, sugar, corn syrups, butter, rye, vanilla, and salt until well blended. Set aside.

FINISH

Heat the oven to 375°F. Roll one ball of dough into two circles 2–3 inches wider in diameter than your pie shell or plate, and place one crust in the pie plate. Reserve the second dough in the refrigerator for a future use.

Using a fork, prick the sides and bottom of the crust at ½-inch intervals. Sprinkle the cooked apples over the pastry. Spread the pecans on top, and pour the egg-syrup mixture over them. Bake in a heated oven for 30–40 minutes, until just set but still slightly loose in the center. (The pie will finish cooking as it cools.) Remove from the oven, and cool on a trivet before serving.

Schnitz Fit

drying apples as Tootie's forebears did was once a common means of preservation. Farmers sliced apples thin, sandwiched them between window screens, and stored them in full sun. They shaved apples and laid them on the tin roofs of outbuildings. They even cored and chunked apples and tossed them on the decks of junked cars to dry.

Many of those dried apples ended up in fried pies. Today, most makers of fried pies—including the two Tennessee women whose portraits follow—buy their fruit from commercial dehydrators. There remain, however, a few old-line sources of dried fruit, principally the Pennsylvania Dutch.

Until fairly recently, "dry houses" heated by wooden stoves were common in Pennsylvania Dutch country. A precious few remain. And yet folks thereabouts still call dried apples by their Pennsylvania Dutch moniker: schnitz. Fewer recall the days when schnitz were so popular—and marketable—that they served as a de facto currency.

But the importance of schnitz lives on in Pennsylvania Dutch lore. Witness the poem written by Louis Livingood of Allentown, Pennsylvania:

She sliced the apples that fell down
And spread them out to dry
These were schnitz when they turned brown
And made delicious pie.

FIVE

Deep-Fried Indemnity

Up above Memphis, near the border with Kentucky, roadside vendors hawk fried apple pies tucked in glassine envelopes. Filling stations stock them by the register. Vegetable stands stack them beside flats of tomatoes in the summer, slat baskets of sweet potatoes in the fall. They're omnipresent, like Crock-Pots of boudin in southwestern Louisiana and bags of boiled peanuts in the South Carolina midlands.

Traveling the back roads of America, especially in the Up South and the Midwest, I spy fried pies with regularity. Near Knoxville, Tennessee, I once tasted a fried pie with a distinctive crust that owed its amber color—and no small measure of its flavor—to the use of flat Coca-Cola as the liquid in the dough. I've eaten Mennonite pies in Kentucky, and Amish variants in Ohio that, appropriately enough, tasted just a tad chaster.

In Alabama, somewhere outside Jasper, I once bought a "Sonshine" fried apple pie, wrapped in a crude sleeve. I was in the parking lot, halfway through demolishing the crescent of crust and stewed apples, before I realized that the maker's name was not a misspelling but a testimony of Christian faith.

I have talked to people who call these treats preaching pies, in tribute to their ability to placate a child squirming for escape from a Sunday-morning sermon. I've heard from huntsmen who know the warmth of secreting a hot one in the slash pocket of a tweed jacket on a cold morning. I've heard the plaints of McDonald's aficionados who remember a day when their lozenge-shaped apple pies were fried instead of baked and all was right with the world.

During a recent run through Tennessee, I met two women—and tasted two pies—that offered opportunity for me to move beyond matters of nomenclature and provenance. Their life stories, like that of Tootie Feagan, offer a glimpse at why the act of making apple pie can take on a larger significance. The pies crafted in this corner of Tennessee are not necessarily unique, but I do believe that they are representative of something that approaches profundity.

i von King's husband went in a week. Cancer, they told her. And then he was gone. That was back in 2001. "You can't tell what's coming," she says. "I took something from that. I surely did."

King is in her early seventies. Her hair is gray and silken, her white face furrowed like fine wale corduroy. I stand behind, watching as she rolls out dough with a pin; cuts it into a circle using a coffee saucer as a guide; and, after plopping a tablespoon of stewed apples bottom center, crimps the half-moon closed with a fork and slides it into a cast-iron skillet set over a countertop electric coil. On a typical weekday, she works four hours in the makeshift kitchen at the back of Jerry Kendall's Fruit Market in Union City. During that time, she will make forty pies. Kendall sells her pies for a dollar-fifty, and Ivon gets a dollar for every one sold.

"I have always cooked," she tells me, flipping a browned pie with the aid of two spatulas and sliding it back into the hissing fat. "And I always knew about fried pies. We took them to our school when I was little. The rich children might bring a saltine four-pack and peanut butter and a marshmallow. I thought they were better-off at the time, but there was this one girl always wanting my fried pie. I always had one in my box."

Her brother was the one who suggested she fry pies. He knew that, with her husband gone, Ivon would need money to supplement her Social Security income. "The Amish folks around here sell [fried pies] on a route, delivering them from place to place," Ivon tells me. "But I didn't want to move around. This place suits me well," she says, looking back over her shoulder past me, eyeing the concrete floor and particle-board ceiling of the fruit shed.

When the pie turns the shade of a timeworn penny, Ivon scoops it from the skillet. After blotting the crust with a paper towel, she sets it on the counter before me. If I had any sense or self-control I would wait for it to cool. But patience is not *my* virtue. I bite. The crust gives easily, yielding first to an inner layer of softer dough and then to a cinnamony goo just this side of applesauce.

Between bites and sharp intakes of cooling air, I tell King how much I like her pie. She smiles. I ask her about the texture of the apples, about how she manages to cook them just so. I ask if she relies upon a special variety of apple, and if the apples she uses are raised in her employer's orchards.

She laughs and points her foot toward a box of Sun-Maid brand dried apples. "That's all we use," she says. "When I was coming up, my parents would core and slice apples and dry them on the tin roofs of old outbuildings. Of course, that was a long time ago, back before my mama passed away. You know she left us when I was a senior in high school. Gone, like my husband. Just gone."

---

fifty or sixty miles southwest of Union City, near the burg of Darden, Margo Hayes fries pies too. Like King, Hayes turned to pies when confronted with an unspeakable loss. But her husband didn't die. She just wished him dead.

"I grew up over in Decatur County, but I'd been living in Nashville for a long time when I came back this way," she tells me, not long after I polish off my first fried apple pie and order a peach pie for good measure. "I had been married twenty-four years when I found out my first husband was keeping another apartment and another woman. That man was taking her the tomatoes I raised in our garden. My tomatoes, raised with my own two hands. Can you imagine that?"

Less than a year passed before she met Jim, her second husband. In 1988, not long after she bought a cinder-block country store out on the highway east of town, he fell through the front door. "He had broke his leg," she tells me. "He broke it bad, and I was there to help get him to the hospital. I helped him get well too. And then I married him."

Today, Jim and Margo Hayes work side by side in the café. She boasts that her fried frog legs "can't be beat," and locals brag on her midday plate lunch. But after I eat two or three of her fried pies—and revel in the distinctive biscuit crust that envelops each—I'm unable to entertain notions of further caloric intake.

It seems that I'm not alone in my passion for her pies. Jim tells me that upon his last count in November 2003, Margo had fried 627,686 pies. (In a manner that makes me think that they're aiming for the *Guinness Book of World Records* or girding for the day when the taxman cometh, he notes each pie sold in an old ledger and can, if inclined, enumerate sales by apple, peach, and chocolate varieties.)

At first, Jim's accounting of fried-pie sales gave me pause. It didn't fit with the notion of quaintness I had ascribed to their enterprise. I figured that since Margo—with her cumulus of white hair and well-rouged face—looks as grandmotherly as Ivon King, she too was just an accidental businesswoman who merely applied what she knew of cookery as a means of supporting herself.

Margo's entrepreneurial ambition reveals itself, though, when I dare pull out my camera and attempt a picture of her crust-rolling technique. "You got ten thousand dollars handy?" she asks, her face fixed with a stern expression. "That's what I charge for a lesson. Ten thousand. Now do you want to get out your checkbook or do you want to put that camera away?" The barest of smiles creases her lips. But I pocket my camera and retreat to a nearby table with a cup of coffee and another pie.

I sit at that table for a while. Margo tells me about her favorite customers, including a man named Pompey Mayo, who would drive over from Lexington to buy a dozen pies at a time. "He hid them under his bed," she recalls. "Ate one every morning and one every night." We talk some more. Though it's obvious she was fond of Mayo, her sentimental impulses are few. Mostly she talks of how she has mastered the art of fried pies, and of how many gross they sell to the truck stop up on the interstate.

S oon I come to know that it would be just as wrong to sentimentalize Ivon King as it would be to trivialize Margo Hayes. Both women, it seems, have come to consider their way with a pie and a skillet to be an indemnity against past—and future—loss. Though operating on far different scales, they know that if all else fails, they can fry pies; they can survive by dishing fried dough and stewed apples.

Coca-Cola Fried Pies

Ivon and Margo would no doubt blanch at my bastardized recipe. But I believe that with the first taste, they would warm to the idea. This crust is a silky wonder—easy to work with and, thanks to the Coca-Cola, just the slightest bit sweet. Coke is a constant in southern cookery. Folks boil hams in it. They spike cakes with the stuff. They even use it as a marinade for beef brisket. And although the use of Coke in pastry dough is less heralded, it's no less tasty.

(continued)

CRUST
- 3 cups all-purpose flour
- 1 teaspoon salt
- 1 cup Coca-Cola, flat

Mix flour, salt, and Coke together, forming a soft dough. Roll out very thin. Using a saucer as a guide, cut rounds. Refrigerate.

FILLING
- ½ pound dried apples
- 1 cup sugar
- 4 cups water
- ½ teaspoon cinnamon

Combine dried apples, sugar, and water in a large pot. Bring to a boil and then reduce to a simmer. Cook for 20 minutes or until water is absorbed. Add cinnamon and set aside.

FINISH
⅓ cup vegetable oil

Put a scoop of filling on the bottom lip of each crust and fold over. With a fork, crimp the edges of each pie.

In a heavy skillet, heat the oil over medium-high. Fry in batches until browned, 3–4 minutes per side. Lift from the skillet with tongs and blot on paper towels.

Hoochie Pie

a year or so back, at the suggestion of my friend Ronni Lundy, I invited brothers Robert Stehling of Hominy Grill in Charleston, South Carolina, and John Stehling of Early Girl Eatery in Asheville, North Carolina, to join me in my hometown of Oxford for a fried-pie cookoff.

Ronni defined the conflict. A fried-pie line separates the Deep South from the Up South, she said. Below the line, fried peach pies prevail. Above, apple pies dominate. The idea of the competition was not so much to name a victor as to cook and eat a mess of pies while elucidating the differences and the similarities.

The brothers Stehling set up shop in an open field and fried their pies in oversized cast-iron skillets set over propane burners. By the second round, a haze of flour enveloped each cook. No clear victor had yet emerged when someone showed up with a jug of moonshine. For reasons that remain unclear to me, a coterie of eaters decided that, before being eaten, representative pies should be broken open and doused with thimblefuls of moonshine. Much tippling and tasting followed until, by general consensus, John's apple pies were declared the best vehicle for hooch.

At the time, I thought moonshine apple pie would always be the most curiously delicious pastry to cross my lips. And then I met Señor Pie, whose story follows.

SIX

Hail Señor Pie,
King of the Truck Stop

Pie lovers of Albuquerque, New Mexico, know Scot Robinson as Señor Pie. They know that the seventy-eight-year-old bakes desserts of peculiar local pedigree: apple pies spiked with fiery green chiles, and cherry pies stoked with smoky chipotles. They know that Señor Pie considers chiles the New Mexican equivalent of salt and pepper, accents that enliven but, if used judiciously, do not overwhelm. What many of them don't know is that this man is a visionary, a seer of pie.

I didn't know him at all until, on a tip from a pie-mad friend, I jetted to Albuquerque, bound for his bunkerlike brick storefront near Kirtland Air Force Base. "Imagine this scenario," Señor Pie, a barrel-gutted Air Force veteran, tells me upon our introduction. "It's the night before Thanksgiving. A million truck drivers are speeding home for the holiday. They know they can't arrive empty-handed, so these million truckers, they gear down and pull in at the nearest truck stop. They fill up their rigs with diesel, and fill up their thermoses with coffee. And since they know that the apple pies we make for truck stops across the country are as good as homemade—maybe even better—they buy a pie to take home to their family."

Señor Pie—his voice gravelly, his eyes ablaze—warms to his fantasy, but he's losing me. I'm eyeing an apple pie that cools atop a glass-fronted pastry case. "Imagine those truckers buying pies on the night before Thanksgiving," he says, as I trace the cinnamon-scented vapor trails that spiral ceiling-ward. "In thousands of truck stops across America, they're doing right by their family, bringing a pie home for the Thanksgiving feast. That would be the first time anyone ever sold one million pies in one day. I'm the man to do it, and I'll do it by selling my pies to real Americans, to blue-collar workers. I figure we've gone too long without it."

As for me, I figure I've gone too long without a bite of his pie. Instead of waiting for my host to offer a seat—much less a fork—I reach for a slice. Señor Pie nods his assent, and, as he chatters on, I chomp down. I taste cinnamon, and a hint of vanilla, and the crisp sweetness of what I guess to be Golden Delicious apples. True to Señor Pie's reputation for subtlety in baked goods, I don't feel the heat on my tongue. At least not at first. Instead, I intuit the grassy tang of the chiles, the way it brightens the apple flavor. And when the heat finally comes, it sneaks across my palate on tiptoe. I remain dubious about whether truckers will adopt the green-chile apple pie as their own, but Señor Pie knows by the smile that creases my face and the tiny pearls of sweat that bead my brow, *I* am an unqualified convert.

Over the course of a five-day ramble about Albuquerque and Santa Fe, I meet sushi chefs who swathe futomaki in a blanket of pickled green chile; pizza makers who smother crusts with mozzarella, marinara, and roasted green chile; and candy makers who dust pistachios with powdered chile. But each cook, each dish, falls short of the Señor Pie ideal.

The only possible analogue I find is in the green-chile cheeseburgers that are ubiquitous hereabouts. But even the luxurious drape of two emerald-colored lobes on a burger capped with cheddar can seem a kind of self-conscious attempt to claim *terroir* for a dish that was not born here amidst piñon and juniper. The green-chile apple pie, on the other hand, does not fall victim to the slap-a-slab-of-foie-gras-on-it-and-call-it-French instinct now popular among cooks. Nor is it ubiquitous. To my knowledge, green-chile apple pie is served at only a handful of cafés, mostly in New Mexico. And many of those cafés buy their pies from Señor Pie.

i ask Scot how green-chile apple pie came to be. He talks of irrigation, of how fruit trees now thrive on the high desert plains. He talks of the superiority of green chiles raised downstate, of how the sweetness of their flesh and the heat of their seed membranes owe a debt to the typical New Mexican interplay of stifling days and bone-chilling nights. And although he admits that apples and chiles make for curious culinary bedfellows, he does not see their pairing as counterintuitive. In a modern New Mexico, where apples and chiles thrive, he believes their pairing to be inevitable.

Once Scot has exhausted a litany of preferred ingredients, he reveals that while recuperating from heart surgery a couple of years back, he took a gamble after reading a magazine article about how grocery-store bakeries were losing market share. "The problem was that people want scratch pies," he tells me as he rummages for an investment prospectus that details the costs and benefits of putting his pies in interstate truck stops. "They want crust made from real butter. They want a pie that oozes out onto the plate when you slice it."

Scot's tale is not without detours. In the midst of defining what Americans expect in a pie, he embraces a defining paradox: How can pie be the ultimate symbol of matronly devotion and also embody a fluid sexuality? "Those bakeries were selling pie that sliced like cake, that stayed put," he tells me, as he screws his face into a leer. "But everybody wants a generous pie that scoots out from beneath the bedsheets and shows its stuff."

On his sixty-sixth birthday, Scot baked his first pie. Soon after, intent upon developing a signature product, he began work on a green-chile apple pie. "I went looking for this woman down in the town of Truth or Consequences," he says. "I heard that she was famous for green-chile apple pies. I drove all around town, searching for her, asking everybody I saw on the streets. Maybe I just dreamed her up, maybe she vanished into the scrub, but no one had ever heard of her, no one had ever heard of a green-chile apple pie. So I went home and tried baking my own."

t hat was nearly two years ago. It would be an exaggeration to say that Señor Pie has met with unbridled success. Since Scot opened the doors, Señor Pie has garnered no national acclaim. For now, devotees of green-chile apple pie constitute a cult of which I am proud to be a member.

Scot seems to know that he may not realize his turnpike dream while baking only green-chile apple pies. With that in mind, he's expanded his offerings to include Dutch apple pie and cranberry apple pie. And yet, unable to forgo his windmill-tilting, he's also added a peach pie that quivers with habañero.

As an eater in search of great feeds, I hope that Scot does

not go mainstream on me, that he continues experimenting with unconventional tastes. But the philosophical side of me believes that his true calling is not in baking the ultimate pie. (He probably came as close as he is able with the green-chile and apple masterstroke.) No, I'm hoping that he puts his considerable energy behind the truck-stop idea. If he staves off temptations to sacrifice handmade taste for industrial throughput, if he cleaves to his standards and delivers honest-to-God pies to the masses, he may have the potential to up-end the gourmet paradigm, to democratize dessert.

The business might work like this: After considerable expansion of Señor Pie's facilities, Scot begins par-baking pies. He'll use the same butter crust, the same Madagascar cinnamon, the same tree-ripe apples (and, if preferred, the same green chiles), but he'll bake the pies to just short of being done, and then flash-freeze them for transport by refrigerator truck. Scot envisions a scenario wherein the truck drivers of America act as his de facto sales force, delivering pies to the rear of truck-stop kitchens before parking their rigs and ambling through the front door to claim seats at the counter and slices of that same apple pie.

I don't pretend to be a business analyst, but even I can come up with a dozen reasons why Señor Pie's truck-stop distribution system will not work. And yet, as I write these words, Scot's business plan is close at hand and my checkbook lies open. According to his analysis, I can purchase a 1 percent share in his limited partnership for $1,250. In return, I will reap one percent of net profits. Maybe I'm addled, but I'm thinking that I might put my money where my mouth is. Call it a philosophical investment instead of a financial one, but I'm thinking about sending Señor Pie a check.

Green with Chile Envy Pie

Señor Pie is particular about his green chiles. And after baking a pie made with the canned stuff available in my local grocery, my wife and I understand why. Canned chiles give off a slightly metallic whang. The scent is not overpowering, but it's there, no doubt about that. A few weeks later, we baked another pie. That time we surfed the web for a good source and splurged on some frozen green chiles from Hatch, New Mexico. They made all the difference, perfuming the pie with a scent that bordered upon floral. My advice? Splurge.

CRUST

Use one of the recipes on pages 10, 20, 39, or 78.

(continued)

FILLING

- 5 large Granny Smith apples
- ½ lemon, juiced
- ½ cup dark brown sugar
- 1 tablespoon all-purpose flour
- 1 teaspoon cinnamon
- 1 teaspoon vanilla
- ½ teaspoon salt
- ¼ teaspoon freshly ground nutmeg
- 1 tablespoon hot green chiles, chopped

Peel and slice apples. In a bowl, mix apples with lemon juice, dark brown sugar, flour, cinnamon, vanilla, salt, and nutmeg with your hands. Add the chiles and stir with a fork.

FINISH

- 1½ tablespoons butter
- white of 1 egg
- 1 tablespoon sugar

Heat the oven to 375°F. Roll the dough into two circles that are 2–3 inches wider in diameter than your pie shell or plate. Place one crust in the pie plate. Mound the filling atop the crust and dot with nubbins of butter. Cut a central vent in the top crust.

Place over the filling and crimp the edges. Glaze the top crust with egg white mixed with 1 tablespoon of water. Sprinkle with sugar. Bake at 375°F for 15 minutes. Reduce heat to 350°F and bake for another 45 minutes or so.

A Cut Above

Señor Pie is an ecumenical baker. He foretells a day when apple pie will be a kind of universal language among people of all stripes. His kinsmen are everywhere and historical examples abound.

"Apple pie is always in style," wrote a columnist for the Portsmouth, New Hampshire, *Herald* in 1900. "Go into a restaurant and ask for a 'cut of standard' and the waiter will bring you a piece of apple pie. He knows what standard apple pie is. There are times in the year when other kinds make a spurt and run on ahead a little, but apple pie keeps jogging on, and by and by it overtakes them."

It's as if Americans share a palate, a taste for apple pie. Some, like Paul Myers, whose story follows, can cite chapter and verse on what makes for a good pie. But none is the equal of Henry Ward Beecher, brother of Harriet Beecher Stowe (from whom we will hear much in succeeding chapters). He proclaimed that a pie reached its apogee "while it is yet fluorescent, white or creamy yellow, with the merest drip of candied juice along the edges (as if the flavor were so good that its own lips watered!), of a mild and modest warmth, the sugar suggesting jelly, yet not jellied, the morsels of apple neither dissolved nor yet in original substance, but hanging as it were in a trance between the spirit and the flesh of apple-hood. . . ."

SEVEN

A Man and His Pie

the palate is predisposed to mock our recollections of tastes past."

That's what I said to Paul Myers, in advance
of our rendezvous—though perhaps without
so much eloquence or brevity. I was looking
out for him. I didn't want to be party to his disappointment when the pie he fetishized turned
out to be less luscious than he remembered,
when the crust for which he pined proved to
have all the texture and savor of pasteboard. I
sought to temper his expectations, for I was

reasonably certain that the sliced apple filling of his dreams would not manifest itself in fruit strata nonpareil.

But Paul was undaunted. He told me of how, while a graduate student at Penn State in 1969, he diverted from a hiking trail to stop at an all-night diner in rural Pennsylvania. There he tasted his first platonic apple pie. Paul described the filling of this particular pie as both substantial and loose. He talked of the all-important pocket formed when the apples shrank down and the domed crust rose high, of how the existence of such a pocket marked the pie as superior.

Paul went on to talk of the dark years. He spoke of how, despite valiant efforts, he was unable to locate the diner again. (Cue theme from *The Twilight Zone.*) He told of how for nearly two decades he searched for a similar pie, haunting Pennsylvania Dutch cafés, quizzing small-town bakers about their preferred techniques, eyeballing slices for the telltale prow that results when a well-domed pie is cut with care. As the years passed, Paul began to understand that his search was informed by philosophy as well as gastronomy. The actual taste began to recede from his memory. The quest began to matter more than the grail.

It took a while, but Paul finally got around to the redemptive part of the story, the part wherein, after moving to San Antonio and gaining tenure in the computer science department at Trinity University, he happened upon a cinder-block diner called John L.'s. "It was mystical," he told me. "I was with a friend, standing in line to get lunch. And there it was, on top of the buffet. The same pie I saw on that hiking trip. Through the haze I saw the height of the crust, the pitch of the slice, and I knew it was the real thing."

that mystical moment occurred in 1989. Twelve blissful years of pie eating followed, during which Paul ate untold lunches of chicken-fried steak or chicken chow mein, capped by a couple slices of pie. He came to know Dora Leung, the wife of John L., as a baker without peer—and as a friend. In time, he forgot about that Pennsylvania pie and accepted this Chinese-American woman as his baker of choice.

But in 2001, Dora closed the lunchroom; John L. had died a few years earlier, and Dora could no longer manage the place herself. Though the term of Paul's deprivation would prove to be far shorter this time, the toll upon his constitution was no less dear. He mourned the loss of Dora's pies. And he suffered untold bouts of pomological tremens.

In the winter of 2004, I rang Paul up. News of his peculiar obsession had reached me by way of a common friend. My intent was to facilitate a reunion of pie baker and pie eater.

But Paul was way ahead of me. Yet another Christmas season without Dora's pies had finally taken its toll. He and Dora were in touch and in the midst of plotting a pie-baking session at his house. I pleaded for an invitation and booked a flight to San Antonio.

On the phone, Paul sounds like Marvin the Martian, the cartoon character with a pipsqueak voice and a scrub brush fixed atop his green helmet. In person, Paul doesn't wear a helmet. He looks to be in his early fifties, has the somewhat frumpy bearing of an intellectual who lives in his head, and bleats when something strikes him as funny. All of which is to say, he's charming.

Dora is nearing eighty. Her hair is piled atop her head in a bun, and her glasses slip often from her nose. Years spent on her feet at the stove have reshaped her body in such a way that, when she claims her place in his kitchen, she tilts forward into the counter.

I retreat to the background to watch and listen. And Paul steps in to serve as Dora's sous chef, fetching milk from the refrigerator and flour from the pantry. When her *mise-en-place* is ready, he too withdraws a bit from the action, ceding the kitchen to his guest. From a stool by her side, he scribbles instructions on a legal pad, stopping at crucial junctures to photograph a well-crimped crust, a mound of apple chunks in a drift of sugar, a pie burnished brown by a forty-five-minute berth in a quick oven.

Dora warms to the attention of her student. With each crust rolled, she shares a little more of her life. We learn that her grandfather emigrated from the Canton province of China to California during the Gold Rush and that her father was a cook at San Antonio's Kelly Air Force Base during

World War I. By the time she retrieves one of the apple pies from Paul's wall oven, we know that, after marrying in 1951, she and John Leung opened a grocery store. Workers at the nearby linen plant bought slices of lunch meat and white bread for lunch. But her customers began to ask for more substantive midday meals. By 1973, grocery begat café. "I don't remember quite when I started making pies," she says. "It just seemed a natural, something we should serve to the people who ate with us. We were already used to cooking everything for everybody.

"Monday was chow mein," she recalls. "Tuesday was spaghetti. You could get fried rice with enchiladas on a combination plate if you wanted. Apple pie seemed like the right thing to serve with everything. And that apple-pie crust was good for empanadas and for chicken pot pies too."

I observe Paul as Dora talks. He listens closely to her story. Or perhaps I should say that he listens closely when he's not stabbing a knife into a burning hot pie and peeling back the crust to admire the telltale pocket. Watching him flit about the kitchen like a robin with a mouthful of worms, I know that my opening admonishment was needless.

Paul is a man sated, a man at peace. By way of tasting her pie, by way of learning her recipe, his quest is over, his denouement near. Paul's palate does not mock his recollections. It affirms them. Just as his audience with Dora affirms for him—and me—the power of apple pie to span chasms delineated by race and color and class.

Paul's Fantasy Pie
with Biscuit Bowl Crust

Dora Leung's piecrust recipe relies upon a technique employed by some biscuit bakers. She makes a kind of drop crust by mixing oil and milk into a bowl of flour. As opposed to many other recipes, this technique does not rely upon chilled ingredients or exacting measurements. The filling is also straightforward, a paean to the crisp goodness of a Granny Smith.

CRUST

- 3 heaping cups all-purpose flour
- 1 teaspoon salt
- ⅔ cup canola oil
- ⅔ cup milk, plus 1 tablespoon for glaze

In a large bowl, mix the flour with the salt. In a liquid measuring cup, pour ⅓ cup of the canola oil and ⅓ cup of the milk. Pour the oil and milk into the flour by hand and gather into a tacky ball. (Almost by its own volition, it will come into a kind of ball, but you'll need to spank it a bit to bring it into a true form.) Remove the first ball and set it aside. Pour in next ⅓ cup each of milk and oil; again gather into a ball. (You will leave behind a good bit of flour in the bowl.) Lay down a sheet or three of newspaper. Lay a sheet of wax paper atop that. Place one of the balls of dough in the center and cover with another sheet of wax paper. Lay down a second blanket on newspaper and wax paper, and repeat.

FILLING

- 6 Granny Smith apples, cored, peeled, and sliced
- 1 lemon, juiced

Fill a large bowl with the apples. Pour lemon juice on top. Fill the bowl with water. Set aside for 15 minutes.

FINISH

- ¾ cup sugar, plus one tablespoon
- ½ teaspoon cinnamon
- 4 tablespoons unsalted butter

Drain the apples. Working from the center and pushing out, roll the first ball of dough into circles just larger than the pie plate. Repeat with the second ball. Place the bottom pastry in the plate. Mound the apples into the pastry. Add the ¾ cup of sugar and a

(continued)

pinch of flour. Blanket with cinnamon. Scatter six pats of butter on the apples. Place this crust atop the apples. Cut six steam vents in top crust. Glaze the top crust with a thin film of milk and then sprinkle with remaining sugar. Bake in a 400°F oven for 45 minutes, or until golden.

Pie Jockey

Paul Myers and Jimmy Malone are of far different temperaments. Paul is a seeker, the quiet sort. Jimmy, on the other hand, has a bully pulpit at his disposal. But both valorize apple pie and the people who bake the good stuff.

As the cohost of the Lanigan and Malone show on Cleveland's 105.7 FM, Jimmy has emerged as a kind of drive-time arbiter of apple pie. On weekday mornings, he picks up the phone, calls a local restaurant, and asks if they serve apple pie. If they don't, he berates them. Not in the manner of a shock jock, mind you, but he does question their palate, their common sense, their allegiance. On the other hand, if Jimmy likes what he hears, he invites the chef into the WMJI studio for an interview and tasting.

Over the years, Jimmy has built a reputation for brooking no nonsense in matters of pie. If only Jimmy had been by my side, I might not have pitched a solo drunk in Celebration— I bet he would have matched me beer for beer.

EIGHT

Freezer Case Piejinks

arly into my quest for peace, love, and apple pie, a packet of materials from the American Pie Council arrives in my mailbox. They want me, little ol' me, to be a judge of the National Pie Championships, held each spring during the Great American Pie Festival at the Disney-fabricated tribute to small-town America known as Celebration, Florida. I picture myself sitting high on a dais, holding forth on pie theory. Or maybe sequestered in a basement, choosing among handcrafted apple pies, before triumphantly emerging with the best.

Delusions aside, the implicit promise is that over the course of a weekend spent tasting and judging, I might survey the state of apple-pie affairs. (I also see the contest as a potential shortcut, a way to taste the pies of, say, the Dakotas, without making the trip.) Though I know any festival staged at the town of Celebration might shine with a veneer of faux wholesomeness, I never suspect that my weekend gig will offer a glimpse at the dark side of pie.

I t's two on a Friday afternoon when, after negotiating my way through Cleaver-dense neighborhoods of zero-lot-line bungalows, I arrive at the epicenter of Celebration. I'm ravenous, having skipped lunch in anticipation of the all-you-care-to-eat feed advertised as the "Never Ending Pie Buffet." I'm also a bit anxious. That might explain why, after dodging a stilt-walking Uncle Sam, a tricycle-cum-piano pedaled by Musicale Mark, and a couple of folks on those infernal Segways, I trip over the backdrop for a dogleg putt-putt course complicated by key lime pie and turtle pie obstacles.

I keep expecting someone to greet me, to welcome the judge and his palate. At the very least, I figure I might score a golf-cart shuttle through the crowds or a key to the special judges-only hospitality suite. But no one at the registration booth has heard of me. No comp tickets to the Never Ending Pie Buffet are reserved in my name. Feeling petulant, I pay my five bucks and streak for the clutch of tents at the apex of Market Street.

Instead of studying my choices, I sidle to the table with the shortest line and snag a wedge-shaped plastic box. The box squawks in my hands as I jimmy the lid and retrieve my slice from its hermetic berth. I plunge a plastic fork through the top crust. Curiously, the fork meets real resistance just beneath the surface, the tines bowing. The damn thing is frozen.

Some pie aficionados prize filling with real crunch. My first Celebration slice delivers that and more. This stuff has the mouthfeel of slush and rock salt shoveled from a midwinter roadway. I'm crestfallen. (Or should I say crustfallen?)

I look around me, hoping for a sign, a promise of pie that was not born on an assembly line. But I find none. In time, it dawns on me that I am surrounded by corporate minions pimping freezer-case pies. Entenmann's, Mrs. Smith's, Edward's, and Sara Lee: all the big guns of the frozen-pie industry are assembled. Though I will taste a number of pies over the course of the weekend that are piping hot instead of slushy-cold, I may never recover from the realization that I have been played for a fool. I've flown to Florida—at my own expense, I might add—to taste the same pies that my local grocer stocks, the very same pies that I wouldn't cross the aisle to purchase.

The implications are myriad: Have the freezer-case folks hit upon the perfect solution for Americans who still recognize apple pie as a symbol of our collective identity, but are unwilling—or perhaps unable—to devote a couple hours to prep work and baking? In paying homage to apple pie's significance, have we rendered it an artifact—better suited to being shellacked and mounted than eaten? Have the freezer-case folks recognized our complicity and co-opted our symbol, reducing it to nothing more than a commodity?

I take some solace in knowing that I am not the first American to turn grumpy when pondering the prospects for great apple pie. As it is with seemingly all things of culinary merit and literary pretension, M. F. K. Fisher was there first. "I try to stay positive about several American institutions, including apple pie," she wrote. "But it is hard not to make firm and even derisive statements about what is fobbed off on us just because we seem to have a compulsive craving for the dish. How dare the local [soda fountain] display, much less sell, what I see boldly cut onto plates on glass shelves behind the fair-tressed serving maid? What good will a scoop of vanilla ice cream lend it? The crust is inedible, like slippery cardboard on the bottom and sugared newsprint on top. The apples are canned vintage, embalmed for posterity in a rare chemical syrup."

i toss my slice in the trash and cast about for a diversion. It's time for a drink. I take refuge in what passes for the local den of iniquity, Sherlock's of Celebration. After drowning my disappointment with a couple of beers, I return to the festival. Turns out that Main Street USA looks better with a buzz on. I look for coconspirators, for fellow travelers inclined to poke sharp sticks at this false pageant. I even concoct a daydream wherein I'm joined by Hunter S. Thompson, whom I find leaning against a lamppost, a flask of Wild Turkey jutting from his back pocket.

But reality—and the quest for apple pie—calls. I wander among the exhibitors, bound for the central stage where, against the backdrop of Town Center Lake, I make out an Up With People–style chorus of fresh-faced kids. They're singing "I'm a Yankee Doodle Dandy" to a drum machine backbeat and prancing about like converts to a peculiar civic religion.

I listen as they race through a patriotic repertoire that includes "You're a Grand Old Flag" and "America the Beautiful" and "This Land Is Your Land." On my right stands a woman wearing a crocheted sweater set, her bosom crowned by a battery-operated brooch that proclaims, marquee style, I LOVE PIE! On my far left stands a crew-cut man. His left forearm boasts a temporary cherry-pie tattoo, which, owing to the faint drizzle now falling, is dissolving into a pool on the underside of his elbow. When I hear the opening bars to that song by Don McLean, the one that shall remain nameless, I flee the stage. My buzz is nearly gone.

there's no doubt about it: The short walk through the streets of Celebration has called forth the cynic in me. My time in Celebration helped cement the hypothesis that animated my quest. It goes something like this: If I am to understand how apple pie functions as an icon of American culture, if I am to ponder why it often serves as a proxy for the American ideal, I need to plumb the bad as well as celebrate the good. After all, where is it written that a meditation on apple pie need be an exercise in easy adoration?

Apple pie is a durable icon with resonance that breaches all manner of social divides. Cases in point: While in New York on a research trip, I once saw Jerry Falwell on television, invoking apple pie and motherhood in a defense of so-called traditional values. The next morning, while combing the collections of the New York Public Library, I came upon a back issue of *Mom's Apple Pie,* the newsletter of the Lesbian Mothers National Defense Fund. As Whitman might have put it, *Apple pie, you contain multitudes.*

though my second day in Celebration will offer redemptive tastes that span the continuum from crumb-topped and homemade to jalapeño-spiked and professionally produced apple pies, I cannot shake what I saw and tasted in my first few hours at the Great American Pie Festival. And you don't yet know the worst of it. When I make my way over to the Kids' Creation Station, I find a clutch of women bent over a row of folding tables. At their sides and in their charge are six or eight children receiving instruction in the fine art of pie making.

At least they are teaching the tykes to roll out crust. But when the time comes to add the filling, there is no talk of apples, no instruction in preferred thickeners and sweeteners. Beneath each table sits a thirty-eight-pound industrial tub of goo that shakes and shimmies like apple aspic harvested from some alien plane. It seems that all one need do is scoop a mess of said filling into a pie shell, clamp a second shell on top, and place the commodity in a 350-degree oven. That, it seems, is how they do it down Celebration way.

On the walk back to Sherlock's, I hear the Up With People singers launch into a reprise of "America the Beautiful." I quicken my step, and upon reaching the bar, order another beer. I figure a fellow had best steel himself before pondering the dark heart of apple pie.

Hypocrite Pie

I planned to end this chapter with instructions for doctoring a frozen pie. In Apple Pie Perfect, *Ken Haedrich details such a doctoring. But then I came upon a recipe for something called Hypocrite Pie in Beth Tartan's* North Carolina & Old Salem Cookery. *It struck me then, and it strikes me now, that a taste of hypocritical pie might be just the thing to top off my days in Celebration. By the way, Tartan says*

(continued)

that the name of this pie refers to the false impression given by the custard topping, which hides the substantial layer of apples lurking beneath. I've toyed with her recipe a good bit, using buttermilk custard instead of a more traditional milk version.

CRUST

Use one of the recipes on pages 10, 20, or 39.

FILLING

- 6 tablespoons butter
- 3 tart apples, peeled, cored, and sliced
- 1 cup white sugar
- ½ teaspoon ground cinnamon
- 2 eggs
- 1 teaspoon vanilla
- 1 tablespoon all-purpose flour
- 1 cup buttermilk

Heat the oven to 300°F. Melt 2 tablespoons of the butter in a skillet. Add apples, ¼ cup of the sugar, and the cinnamon. Cook over medium heat for 4 to 5 minutes, until the apples are tender. Set aside.

In a large bowl, combine the remaining 4 tablespoons of softened butter with the remaining ½ cup of the sugar. Beat until creamy. Beat in the eggs one at a

time. Mix in the vanilla and flour. Pour in the buttermilk and beat until silky.

FINISH

Working from the center and pushing out, roll the
dough into circles just larger than the pie plate. Repeat. Place one crust in a pie pan and prick the bottom
with a fork. Save the other crust for a future use.
Spoon the apples into the crust. Pour the buttermilk
custard over top, ensuring that it thoroughly covers
the apples. Bake for 50 to 60 minutes, or until a knife
inserted in the center comes out clean.

One Pie If by Land, Two If by Sea

incidentally, I don't reject the possibility that large-scale
production facilities can turn out a great pie. That's what
my friend Señor Pie of Albuquerque plans to do. Indeed, you
could go so far as to argue that only after untold sessions of
dough rolling is a cook capable of a superior crust. Large-
scale production doesn't risk my ire until it begets industrial
throughput.

Just the other day, I came across a reference to a pie concern that operated in Connecticut in the mid-1800s. Amos Munson was the principal. In 1844 he opened a bakery in New Haven with the intent of shipping pies by steamboat to New York where, his homesick son said, they longed for "old-fashioned pies." By all accounts, Munson thrived, selling city folk a taste of small-town Connecticut.

In my mind's eye I see Munson's assembly line, staffed by legions of women expert in the craft of pie. On my mind's palate, I taste the apples, the crimson-striped Baldwins, the beautifully lopsided Gravensteins. And in the ledger of my dreams, I note the thousand-pies-per-day pace that Munson met, one hand-rolled crust at a time.

NINE

The Jewel
in God's Pocket

fter that misstep at Celebration, I ponder canceling my trip to Julian, California. But I am determined to explore the
notion that one community might serve as a
citadel of American apple pie. At Celebration,
apple pie matters one weekend each year.
But from what I hear, Julian, a onetime gold-
mining town northeast of San Diego, worships
yearlong at the shrine of apple pie. So I jet
westward. And after a daylong detour spent

sampling the French fry–stuffed burritos popular along the California coast, I drive inland and uphill.

I first learned of the village during the fall of 2003, when a firestorm raged through the piney woods of southernmost California. It would prove to be the most treacherous fire in the state's history, scorching more than 700,000 acres, destroying more than 2,500 homes, and killing more than twenty people. During the height of the blaze, television networks broadcast footage of efforts to save Julian by setting backfires on country roads, drenching rooftops in torrents of water, and dropping payloads of flame-retardant chemicals from tanker planes.

Vestiges of the blaze are everywhere. Climbing through the foothills, I pass fields of dove-white boulders set, like conceptual sculpture, in a charcoal chaparral. Plywood signs tacked to creosote-swabbed telephone poles proclaim, THANK YOU, FIREMEN! And then I come to Julian. Though more than one-quarter of Julian's full-time residents lost their homes, the village core seems to have survived intact.

Celebration is a bauble, a collection of dollhouses assembled by a developer to *look* as if it were built decades ago. Julian, on the other hand, has a past as well as a present. Now, don't get me wrong—Julian caters to tourists. The place is lousy with bed-and-breakfast inns. Horse-drawn carriages clip clop down the streets. Tour companies offer overnight llama treks. And the local museum displays a collection of mignonette lace that may be the grandest in the state. But it's readily evident why so many firemen fought so long and hard to save it. Perhaps they recall a time when locals, boastful of the natural beauty that comes with being tucked away in a vale between the Cuyamaca range and Volcan Mountain, called Julian the "jewel in God's pocket."

Life revolves around a four-block stretch of Main Street, flanked by clapboard buildings with stepped façades that recall a back-lot set for the television series *Gunsmoke*. Stand dead center in that street on a weekday morning, and you can conjure the year 1870, when prospectors discovered a rich vein of gold ore. What will not be so readily evident is how, when easily recovered gold deposits began to play out over the next couple of decades, apples—and apple pie—came to the fore.

*a*fter weathering twenty or so years of whipsaw economics common to speculative mining, the raising of apples appealed greatly to the good people of Julian. "Take care of an orchard for five years," read the ads run by mail-order nurseries of the day, "and it will take care of you for the rest of your life." Most come-ons are too good to be true, and this was no exception. The orchardists of Julian were speculators in their own right, gambling that pests would not burrow into their fruit, that markets would grow apace with their capacity to produce crops.

But the fruit they raised was superior. Apples thrived in a

local microclimate defined by dry summers and high eleva-tion. For a twenty-two-year stretch during the late 1800s and early 1900s, Julian apples won top prizes at the Los Angeles County Fair. In 1904, orchardist W. L. Detrick brought home the gold medal for apples from the St. Louis World's Fair. In 1907 the National Pomological Society awarded a Julian grower its medal for the best apples in North America. And in 1909, in recognition of their ascendant cash crop, the local cham-ber of commerce inaugurated a fall Apple Day celebration.

By 1914, local apple ambassador Arthur Juch traveled to fairs and expositions across the country, constructing baroque displays of Bellflowers and Greenings and Baldwins to show-case the spoils of Julian. By mid-century, promoters grew shameless, touting local varieties like the Julian Duchess as "a blonde and blushing darling with a tender skin, sweet and aromatic, a very Lana Turner among apples."

As acreage grew and output climbed, as more and better roads linked the city of San Diego with backcountry villages like Julian, growers worked to expand their reach. By the late 1940s, San Diego was just an hour and a half away, but trans-port costs continued to cut into profits. So some smart soul—whose name is now lost to the ages—decided to sell apple pie instead of apples. The rationale was simple: Why drive truck-loads of apples south to San Diego when we can attract week-end pilgrims *here,* for our apple pie? Let them buy the gasoline; let them drive the route.

In an effort to beat the drum, the chamber of commerce revived Apple Day, which eventually became the kind of event that drew thousands. Soon the women's club was baking pies for sale to tourists. And the chamber of commerce, under the leadership of a fellow named Les Ecklund, established an Apple Pie Club, which, besides baking a surfeit of pastries, concocted a trademark sauce to serve with pie. Some people remember it as a caramel, others recall that it was cream-based, and everyone will tell you it was delicious.

By the 1950s, Julian's mining-town heyday was long past. And the apple industry was maturing, as community endeavor begat commercial competition. During the decade, the Apple Pie Club ran its course. But by then, apple pie had become firmly ensconced as the town's signature dish. The 1954 Apple Day brochure advertisement for Tom's Café heralded JULIAN APPLE PIE in bold type. In 1957, Nola Mae's Pine Café promised HOME MADE PIE. By the 1970s, apple-pie vendors began to displace the old-line businesses of Julian. Hardware stores installed soda fountains. Livery stables begat pastry shops. It was, depending upon your perspective, the beginning of the end or the promise of the future.

i imagine that the Julian of today looks much like Julian of old—except, of course, for the omnipresence of shingles that advertise apple pie. Here, the filling stations stock Gold Rush brand three-packs of Julian jam, and a few bakers even ship pies nationwide. Wandering the streets, I spy no less than eight spots where a fresh-baked slice can be had, including Miner's Diner & Soda Fountain, Mom's Pie House,

Julian Café & Bakery, Apple Alley Bakery, and even Candied Apple Pastry Company, which in a recherché move, deigns to serve apple tarts but nary a pie.

I sample five or six. Truth be told, it's easy to lose track when, for the most part, the pies look as if they were rolled from the same sheet of pastry. The best proves to be a sprightly boysenberry-spiked apple-crumb version, baked by Julian Pie Company. At their secondary location, a little Main Street cottage, I come to know more than the taste of great pie. After taking note of the signs that proclaim TOUR BUSES WELCOME, I begin to think of issues of orchard volume and pie-production capacity. According to what locals tell me, local apple tonnage is now dropping steadily, even as the reputation of Julian apple pie continues to escalate.

When I ask the counterwoman at Julian Pie Company how they deal with this, how they can continue to bake pies made with local apples, she demurs. But when I ask the same question of a docent at the Julian visitor's center, she gives me a matter-of-fact answer. "During a good year, growers can come close to producing what the bakers need," she says. "But during a bad year—or in the dead of winter—those trucks full of cold-storage apples come rumbling up in the middle of the night from Utah and Washington."

I hear no regret in her voice. What I hear instead is a woman who recognizes that, in making a market for their apples, Julian growers and Julian bakers have succeeded beyond their wildest dreams. They have shored up a village, one pie at a time.

Dueling Julian Sauces

No record remains of the sauce that Julian promoters first served with their pies. But I'm not one to let a lack of facts quell speculation. Based upon period taste, here are two archetypal and delicious recipes. Serve them with any of the pie recipes detailed in these pages, except perhaps the Cheese-Straw Apple Pie.

Caramel Sauce

This caramel sauce is based on a recipe in Rose Levy Beranbaum's The Pie and Pastry Bible. *Blair refers to her, with affection and admiration, as Rose Levy Bonbon.*

- 1 cup sugar
- 1 tablespoon white corn syrup
- ¼ cup water
- ½ cup liquid heavy cream, heated
- 2 tablespoons unsalted butter, softened
- pinch of salt
- 1½ teaspoons pure vanilla extract (or rum or bourbon)

(continued)

In a heavy saucepan, stir together the sugar, corn syrup, and water until the sugar is saturated with liquid. Heat, stirring constantly, until the sugar dissolves and the syrup bubbles. Stop stirring and allow it to boil until it turns deep amber. Do not disturb the syrup during this interval. When a candy thermometer registers 380°F, remove it from the heat and slowly—very slowly!—pour the hot cream into the caramel. It will bubble like a witches brew, and, if it pops from the pot, it will burn you like napalm.

Stir with a wooden spoon until smooth, scraping the thick syrup from the pan bottom. If lumps develop, return to the heat and stir. Swirl in the butter. Add the salt. Allow the sauce to cool for 3 minutes. Gently stir in the vanilla extract. Place in a little bowl or pitcher for pie drenching.

Nutmeg Rum Sauce

This is a sauce of my own creation, inspired by the vague memories shared with me by Julian folks.

- 1 egg yolk
- ½ cup sugar
- ½ cup milk
- ½ teaspoon ground nutmeg
- 1 tablespoon dark rum

In a saucepan, beat yolk, sugar, and milk together. Heat until the mixture boils. Cook at a boil for 2 minutes. Remove from the heat, and stir in the rum and the nutmeg. The sauce will thicken as it cools.

Mock It to Me

Common belief holds that mock apple pie is a Depression-era dish, first baked during the 1930s when Ritz crackers debuted. The story goes that at a time when apples were sold on street corners by the unemployed, a mock apple pie make with hoity-toity Ritz became a poor man's indulgence.

The basic recipe—wherein crumbled, seasoned crackers serve as a proxy for an apple filling—is straightforward: Crumble a cup or two of crackers in a pie crust, soak with water and lemon juice, sweeten with sugar, flavor with cinnamon and nutmeg and other traditional spices, crimp down the top crust, and bake for forty-five minutes. It's an odd riff on apple pie, to be sure, but my guess is that it was better than nothing when apples were absent or unaffordable.

Review a selection of older cookbooks and you'll soon note that, though the National Biscuit Company popularized it, mock apple pie is not remotely newfangled. In her 1881 book *What Mrs. Fisher Knows About Old Southern Cooking,* Abby Fisher offered recipes for cracker pie flavored with cloves and cinnamon. Similar was the nutmeg-laced recipe in the *Confederate Receipt Book* of 1863.

Mock apple pie was not, however, a Southern dish born of Civil War deprivation. Among the early advocates was a self-proclaimed California pioneer who, in 1852 when apples sold for a dollar a pound, talked of baking cracker-filled mock apple pies for children "to appease their homesick cravings."

TEN

Apple Pie Oddments

bake enough apple pies for dinner and soon enough you'll be eating apple pie for breakfast. That's how it started. I would return home from a research trip, rhapsodizing about the candied-ginger apple pie at Bread Line in Washington, D.C., or the molasses-rich apple pie at City Bakery in New York City, and a few days later, when the tremens began in earnest, Blair would spank out a crust.

Three-quarters of the pies she baked never made it in this book. Some, like a gorgonzola apple pie, were flights of excess. Others, like a pie pocked with *fleur de sel* caramels, proved tasty but were too quirky to be illustrative of apple pie as savored in America.

Eight slices was the average yield. Blair would eat one, I would eat two, and Jess might nibble at another. Sometimes Blair would deliver slices to a neighbor or a friend, but even when she did that, I woke to find at least one wedge of crust and apples left for me. Early on, I became convinced of the merits of an apple-pie breakfast. Sure, the practice can seem a bit louche, but I believed that history was on my side.

If anyone dared question my morning regimen, I told them that in years past a slice of pie from the previous day's dinner made an ideal breakfast for a farmworker who rose before dawn to milk the cows or feed the chickens, only to return home before a proper breakfast of eggs and salt pork and corncakes could be prepared. And if they dared question my chicken-feeding credentials, I would hit them with the strudel defense: A breakfast slice of apple pie is elementally— if not structurally—the same as a breakfast slice of apple strudel.

he strudel line works for a while. But I know that if I am to defend my new breakfast habit, I must establish either contemporary corroboration or unassailable historical foundation. To confirm that our forebears ate pie for breakfast, I spend a day in the library, perusing books on culinary history and crawling the Web.

And the roots of an apple-pie breakfast do indeed appear to be historical. "As a rule, we made the fire at six in the morning if the wood was not too green," wrote a bachelor New Hampshire correspondent in 1891. "If we could not make the fire go, we would breakfast upon apple pie and milk. . . . The great beauty of an apple pie breakfast, aside from its power to generate indigestion, lies in the fact that it doesn't leave behind it a number of dishes thickly encrusted with ham grease to be cracked with a hammer or melted off over a candle."

A generation or so later, the idea of a breakfast of apple pie still enthralled—and still vexed. "About this matter of eating pie for breakfast of which Vermonters have been accused," wrote Aristene Pixley in *The Green Mountain Cook Book* of 1934, "it must be admitted that at one time the accusation was justified, and even now pie might be found on the breakfast table in the outlying farm districts. It should be realized, however, that there is a great difference between those who rise in the morning, dress and breakfast, and those who rise, put in several hours of heavy labor, and then breakfast."

M. F. K. Fisher had her say in 1969. "Our American fruit pies are, as far as I can tell, unique to our culture," she wrote in *With Bold Knife and Fork*. "And hinterlanders still eat them at breakfast, and what is wrong with that, if the crust be light and the apples and cinnamon and butter a commendable mixture? Why complicate life by combining much the same things all over the table: buttered toast and jam, a bowl of applesauce?"

———

Why indeed? Fisher emboldened me. I figure that, with a little digging in the stacks, I can justify any of my gastronomic inclinations. Which brings me, of course, to the matter of apple pie and cheese. I was raised on a steady diet of the stuff. Never for breakfast, mind you. But at lunch or dinner I thought a wedge of pie was naked if it wasn't crowned with a preternaturally orange slice of cheddar.

When I dive back into the library, I learn that many people consider the pairing to have been popularized in New England. But that's about it. I search for historical accounts, and I find none. Of course, I come across the Eugene Field ditty: "But I, when I undress me / Each night, upon my knees / Will ask the Lord to bless me / With apple pie and cheese." And then there's that bit of New England nonsense, "Apple pie without the cheese / Is like a kiss without the squeeze." But save a few vague references to a birth across the Atlantic in England, I find no signposts, no references of historical or cultural merit. And so I am left with no choice but to travel to New England and engage in what folklorists call participant observation. In other words, I'll watch and listen while I eat.

I wander about Vermont for a couple of days, seeking a café or bakery that serves apple pie with cheese. No dice. No pie with cheese. Little do they know they are violating a state law. According to my friend Marilyn Wilkerson, an expert on the cheeses of Wisconsin, the legislature of Vermont passed a statute in 1999 requiring that restaurants make a "good faith effort" to serve apple pie with, "among other products, a slice of Cheddar cheese weighing a minimum of ½ ounce." Wisconsin passed a similar law in 1935, she tells me with regret—maybe even a tinge of jealousy—"but it was only on the books for a couple of years, and they never specified the variety or the weight of the cheese."

Regardless of the law, I fail miserably. Everyone is polite and quite a few folks tell me that they enjoy a slice of cheddar on their pie from time to time, but I am left with no choice but to conclude that Vermont is populated with scofflaws. Five stops at five cafés, all to no avail. Hungry and frustrated, I bed down at a cheap motel in an itchy nest of sheets.

hope springs eternal on a brisk April morning in Vermont. At the Grafton Village Cheese Company in the hamlet of Grafton, I hit paydirt. Sort of. It seems that the Old Tavern down the road serves slices of apple pie topped with wedges of three-year-old Grafton Village cheddar that, after a run beneath the broiler, express rivulets of butterfat that bubble and pop like errant fondue. Only problem is, the tavern is closed for mud season.

Instead, I hunker down in conversation with Peter Mohn and Chad Bessette of Grafton Village Cheese. We spend a good hour puzzling over the marriage of apple pie and cheese. We talk of the European habit of eating a cheese course before dessert, and of how this habit might have precipitated such a pairing. We speak of nineteenth-century beliefs that held cheese to be, in the words of Catherine Beecher, sister of Henry Ward Beecher and Harriet Beecher Stowe, "a common appendage to the digestion." We finally give up on my query and begin tasting three-, four-, and five-year-old cheeses that, with each year of aging, grow sharper and somehow more rounded, until, at the five-year mark, they reach the height of their potential for betrothal.

I depart the village with a brick of five-year-old cheese in my trunk and drive north in search of more pie bakers. Despite a roster of café and bakery suggestions compiled by Peter and Chad, I fail in each attempt at realizing my platonic ideal. Everyone has apple pie, but no one makes a habit of capping pie slices with cheddar.

After my third attempt, I take matters in my own hands. At Burnham Hollow, a roundhouse provisioner just east of Rutland, I request yet another slice with cheese. I am kindly rebuffed; Burnam Hollow sells no slices and has no cheese. This time, rather than exit hungry, I return to my car, unwrap that five-year-old cheddar, and march right back in the shop.

Baker Mary Traverse hands over a whole pie, still warm from the oven. With my car key, I cut a small wedge of pie free and chip off a splinter of cheese. I place the cheddar atop the slice and pause. When the cheese has relaxed to a point just this side of a puddle, I bite down, savoring the counterpunches of cinnamon and sugar and apples and cheese. The taste is so good that I reach for another slice.

But I pull up short when I realize that I don't yet know where I will wake in the morning. Who knows if I will be able to find a café that serves a proper apple pie? And if I do find such a café, will they have a proper cheddar to lay atop it? In the face of such uncertainty, it seems the better part of valor to conserve my provender.

Rise-and-Shine Pie

A breakfast of apple pie requires no special recipe. I like a double-crust pie, warmed in the oven and topped with either a slice of good cheddar or napped with heavy cream. Of course, you should never heat your pie in a microwave. Those infernal machines destroy crusts, leaving them either desiccated or sweaty. I can't recall which; it's been too long since I made that mistake.

If you really want to live a little, fry up a few patties of smoked sausage and eat those along with your slice. You will no doubt note that the sweetness of the apples plays well off the pork. And if anyone calls you on it, tell them to talk to me. I've got a file at home, brimming with historical recipes for apple pie with gratons of pork.

Call of the Magpie

the word pie may have been borne of the magpie bird. Among the well-reasoned articulations of such a linkage is one found in *Ladyfingers & Nun's Tummies* by Martha Barnette. Her historical rationale is this: Pie has long been a container for a miscellany of ingredients. And so has the nest of the magpie, a bird she deems "notorious" for "collecting various and sundry items and hoarding them."

At first blush, this may smack of fakelore, but Barnette strengthens her argument with a disquisition on Scottish haggis—a sheep stomach stuffed with, among other ingredients, offal and oatmeal. Of course, haggis is, at its core, a kind of pudding. And so is a pie, albeit a pudding contained within a crust. The word *haggis,* Barnette points out, was likely born of *hagges* or *haggis,* obsolete English words for magpie.

While we're at it, I can't help but point out that these linguistic theories offer, by extension, plausible rationale as to why schoolchildren sing of four and twenty blackbirds baked in a pie, why ceramicists often crafted steam funnels for pies in the shape of openmouthed birds, and why bakers often incised patterns called bird tracks in top crusts.

ELEVEN

What It Means
to Be Fluent in Cider

my excursions about New England could not have been timelier. Call me an ingrate, but I arrived bored. There, I said it. I arrived in New England bored by apple pie.

My previous efforts had afforded me tastes of moonshine-goosed pies and chile-spiked pies. Not to mention pies made with Coca-Cola crust, and milkshakes stoked with pureed pies. But most were, at their core, structurally and texturally the same. They were emblematic, iconic, typical. And I had grown tired of the typical. I craved different textures, different tastes.

I wanted to delve more deeply into apple pies that flout the sliced-apples-between-two-crusts paradigm. And I figure New England is as good a place as any for pondering flouted pies. So, after leaving Rutland, I drive the length and breadth of the state, only to be pulled back into the general orbit of Grafton by an invitation from Tina and Willis Woods, who make boiled cider in the timberlands beyond Weathersfield.

W e were back-to-the land hippies," explains Willis, a bearded man who, like his kind-faced wife, exudes a youthful vigor, a kind of salt-of-the-earth resolve. "I was a conscientious objector during the Vietnam War," he tells me as we sip coffee at their dining room table. "There were a lot of people like us. Tina went to Bennington; I went to Dartmouth. . . . For a brief period in time, it wasn't so odd to go to an Ivy League school and then tramp off into the woods. The difference was, when all the other hippies got bored growing lettuce, we had a reason to stick around."

Augustus Aldrich was eighty-two when the twenty-two-year-old newlyweds accepted work on his farm. The plan was for the Woodses to stay a few years, to help Willis's aged cousin fix up the place. Maybe Willis would plane a little timber, or tack up a few sap buckets in the sugarbush. And then they would be on their way. But not long after his eighty-sixth birthday, Augustus set out to hike Mount Katahdin, the tallest peak in Maine. He never came home. (In tribute, Willis fixed one of the old man's calling cards to a wall in the farm office. Among the vocations and avocations listed thereon are skier, runner, photographer, mapmaker, explorer, climber, and mountaineer.)

Before they knew what they were doing, Willis and Tina bought fifty acres and a circa-1798 farmhouse from Augustus's children. They also inherited one of the last cider evaporators in New England. "Best as I can tell, the Aldriches first made cider in 1882," says Willis. "They worked a water-powered sawmill from the 1860s until the early 1880s. By then, most of the land had been cleared, the timber harvested. Vermont was considered built out then, and the population started declining. But instead of moving west like a lot of farmers were doing, they converted the sawmill to a cider mill."

I was somewhat fluent in cider before visiting the Woods family. I knew that for much of the colonial era and beyond, fermented apple cider was the preferred American refresher. Thanks to the kindness of writer Frank Browning, whose family tends an apple orchard in Kentucky, I also knew—after a bottle or three—that a well-crafted cider has all the nuance, all the fruit and flair and structure of a great wine. But I didn't know diddly-squat about boiled cider or its reductive kin, cider jelly.

Turns out that I am not alone, for even in 1974, when Tina and Willis bought the farm, boiled cider was considered an anachronism. "I think boiled cider was in vogue from the 1880s through the 1920s," Willis tells me as Tina pulls a single-crust pie from the nearby woodstove. Tina cuts and serves, and I soon lose track of what Willis is saying. Maybe he says something about how his family once sold barrels of boiled cider to a soft-drink manufacturer down South. Maybe he says a hosanna over the pie. Upon first bite, I do.

The body of Tina's pie is custardlike, the top ringed in apple slices. "I added sour cream to our regular recipe," says Tina. "Dairy can sometimes temper the boiled cider." With that first taste, the sharpness of boiled cider combusts across my palate. It's not fizzy like a hard cider drink, of course, but the taste is pleasantly abrasive, in the same way that a young wine can taste tannic, almost chewy. When I tell Tina that it's among the best pies I have ever tasted, she counters that the sour cream has rendered it a bit soupy. No matter, at a time like this, when I'm seeking diversion, it tastes downright ambrosial.

more than two hours have passed since I first took a seat at the Woodses' table. I've eaten well. I've learned a bit about the making of boiled cider, of how sweet cider is boiled down to one-seventh its original volume. I know now that cider jelly, which Willis also makes, is boiled down to one-ninth its original volume. And I've learned that Augustus Aldrich liked to smear cider jelly on fresh-from-the-fryer donuts.

What's more, I learn that the next generation of Woodses

are of like political minds. I've learned that their niece, who aspires to run the farm one day, can't ever seem to make it back home when it's time to boil the maple sap. It seems she's too busy marching in protest of George W. Bush's Vietnam. Though Willis hopes her distraction won't prove permanent, he appreciates her youthful vigilance.

It's nearing midday when Willis and I amble out the side door, bound for the shed where he presses apples for cider and boils sap for syrup. He talks of the frugal impulse behind the making of cider, of how culls and drops (blemished and windfall apples) are repurposed using a nineteenth-century ratchet press. And once we gain the shed he shows me how he wraps ground apples in monstrous tarps, how he stacks layer upon layer upon layer of those tarps to form a wild Dagwood sandwich, and then engages ancient gears and "turns down" the press's beech wood beam that will, in an hour's time, express the sweet cider.

Eventually our conversation loops back around to the golden days of boiled cider. We talk of the Shakers, who boiled cider for their famous applesauce. Willis tells me, as we peer down at the coffin-shaped wood-fired evaporator, that a locally popular version of mincemeat once called for venison cut from deer necks, moistened and bound with boiled cider. I tell Willis that he's describing dishes that are, by their very nature, antiquated. Willis listens and smiles, and allows that the true reason boiled cider fell out of favor might be the vicissitudes of the American diet.

"Maybe boiled cider—like hard cider—was a casualty of

the temperance movement," Willis says. "But it may just have been that tastes changed. Maybe people came to think that boiled cider was too tart, too strong. Maybe that notion will change again. . . . When we first moved here, the people who bought boiled cider had blue hair. Now we're selling it to yuppies. Mind you, I'm not complaining," he says, as he hands over two quart jars and counts out my change.

Back-to-the-Land Boiled-Cider Pie

Boiled cider is integral to this recipe. If you're feeling frisky, you could boil down some sweet cider until it's reduced to one-seventh of its original volume, and then proceed with the recipe. But since Willis Woods has a six-generation head start on you, chances are your rendition won't turn out as well as his. The better course is to dial 802-263-5547. More than likely, Willis or Tina will answer the phone and sell you a quart for ten bucks and change. Of course, you could also try their website, www.woodscidermill.com, where Tina has posted a number of other recipes, but that's an awfully impersonal way to get your hands on heirloom booty.

CRUST

Use one of the recipes on pages 10, 20, or 39.

FILLING

- 1 cup boiled cider
- 2 eggs, beaten
- ¾ cup whole milk
- ⅓ cup maple syrup or brown sugar
- 3 tablespoons all-purpose flour

In a deep bowl, whisk all the ingredients together until well incorporated.

FINISH

Heat the oven to 350°F. Roll the dough into two circles that are 2–3 inches wider in diameter than your pie shell or plate. Place one crust in the pie plate. Save the other crust for another use in the refrigerator. Pour the filling into the piecrust and bake, in a 350°F oven, for 40 to 50 minutes or until a knife inserted in the center of the pie comes out clean.

À *la Mode de Massachusetts*

t he parsing of apple pie lore and language can get a mite fussy. In his book *The Eaten Word,* Jay Jacobs writes that *à la mode* "is a meaninglessly incomplete formulation, a sort of linguistic coitus interruptus that locks French and English in an awkward embrace without issue. In its legitimate usage, *à la mode* (in the style) would be preceded by a French noun and followed by *de* (of) and someone or someplace or other, as in *tripes à la mode de Caen*."

Reading along, I embrace his condemnation of the ill-considered and constructed expression until, in the very next sentence, he dares proclaim, "Whatever pie *à la mode* is in the style of, is anyone's guess."

Face facts, Mr. Jacobs: You know very well that in your native land, pie served *à la mode* is gobbed with vanilla ice cream. You know that, just as I know that an especially tart pie—like the boiled-cider pie in the last chapter or the Marlborough pie in the next chapter—tastes best when swaddled in cream, whether that cream be served hot from a teat or frozen from a tub.

TWELVE

The Marlborough
(Wo)man

i brought along a book, published in 1869, to read on my New England travels. For those enamored of pie, it should be considered a primary text. *Oldtown Folks* is the title, and Harriet Beecher Stowe is the author. I was familiar with her work as a novelist and abolitionist, but with the exception of an oft-quoted phrase about how, when introduced to America, pie "burst forth into untold genera and species," I was unaware of her peculiar obsession with pie.

It seems she was batty for the stuff. And her battiness reached its peak right around Thanksgiving. "The making of pies at this period assumed vast proportions that verged upon the sublime," she wrote in recollection of her early-nineteenth-century childhood celebrations. "Pies were made by forties and fifties and hundreds, and made of everything on the earth and under the earth. . . . Pumpkin pies, cranberry pies, huckleberry pies, cherry pies, apple pies, Marlborough-pudding pies—pies with top crusts, and pies without—pies adorned with all sorts of fanciful flutings and architectural strips laid across and around, and otherwise varied, attested the boundless fertility of the feminine mind, when let loose in a given direction."

I am besotted by her enthusiasms. I read on, as she breathes life into a New England kitchen where "the jolly old oven roared and crackled in great volcanic billows of flame, snapping and gurgling as if the old fellow entered with joyful sympathy into the frolic of the hour; and then, his great heart being once warmed up, he brooded over successive genera-tions of pies and cakes, which went in raw and came out cooked, till buteries and dressers and shelves and pantries were literally crowded with a jostling abundance."

And thinking ahead to the bitter winter that awaited Stowe and her kin, I take solace in knowing that surplus pies were preserved in what she termed a "great cold northern chamber . . . where ice and frost reigned with undisputed sway." There, frozen solid, "and thus well-preserved in their icy fetters, they formed a great repository for all the winter months; and the pies baked at Thanksgiving often came out fresh and good with the violets of April."

i n a more sober moment, I take stock of her words. If you ignore the breathless flush of her language and the mechanics of her cookstove and deep freeze, you have the makings of a recognizably modern Thanksgiving. Notwithstanding one exception: Who ever heard of Marlborough-pudding pie?

I call around. Though a few people have heard of it, no one claims a command of said pie. No one except Deb Friedman, the foodways expert at Old Sturbridge Village, a nineteenth-century living-history community in central Massachusetts. Every Web reference brings me back to her. Every book index pulls me into her orbit. So I phone her, secure an appointment, and, in a move that would make Columbo proud, ask, at our conversation's denouement, "When I come to see you, will you tell me how to bake a Marlborough-pudding pie?"

God bless her; Deb Friedman says yes. She'll bake one for me; in fact she bakes Marlborough-pudding pies all the time. "Of course I make it for Thanksgiving," she tells me. "My family demands it, but I also make it when the soccer club has a bake sale. All the other mothers bring brownies or cookies. They'll have twenty pans of brownies displayed on one of those folding tables. And my Marlborough pie. It's one of the foods from the nineteenth century that translates easily to the modern day."

for the longest time, New Englanders called the object of my growing obsession pudding. As in, "Would you like another plate of Marlborough pudding?" But according to Deb, it was then—and remains today—what we know as pie, albeit not a double-cruster bursting with sliced apples. Marlborough pie is a comparatively austere single-crust variation, filled with a lemon- and sherry-spiked custard of pureed apples and eggs.

We talk in her office, in a concrete bunker of a building, on the backside of Old Sturbridge Village. An egg-yellow Marlborough pie sits on Deb's secretary, just out of my reach. Her bulletin board is chockablock with memos detailing the latest theories on hearth cookery and back issues of *Food History News*. Her bookcase is stacked with academic tomes like *Albion's Seed* by David Hackett Fischer, *The Tomato in America* by Andy Smith, *Our Own Snug Fireside: Images of the New England Home 1760–1860* by Jane Nylander. The past lives in those books. And it lurks in the hallway where every few minutes a woman in a bonnet scuttles by, on the way to greet a throng of schoolchildren intent upon learning the intricacies of the loom or experiencing the spark and clamor of the blacksmith's forge.

Out in the village, along the dirt lanes and inside the clapboard houses, the year is 1830. As Deb and I talk, she eases into character. Her transformation is not purposeful. It is slight, subtle. When we began our conversation, she talked of *recipes* for Marlborough pie, but now she has taken to using the antiquated term, *receipts*. And somewhere along the way, my pie became her pudding. Though Deb has not donned a bonnet, she has assumed the attitudes and prejudices of the day.

We talk of how Marlborough pudding came to be popular in the early 1800s. "Eating seasonally was not always about eating foods at the peak of their freshness," she tells me. "To eat seasonally at Thanksgiving was, in part, to eat foods that were on the verge of spoiling. Pearl onions didn't keep long. Neither did some apples. And the apples we used for Marlborough pudding were not the best. Those were stored in sand in a root cellar. The ones with slight blemishes might be sliced and dried. The worm-riddled ones, the ones close to rot, those are the ones we crushed and strained through a horsehair sieve. That way the garbage and worms would stay behind and the rest would be made into Marlborough pudding."

We talk of how and why Marlborough pudding fell out of favor by the close of the century. I wonder aloud about whether it was a casualty of the American tendency toward excess and away from frugality. But Deb demurs. "You see the same principle at work with orange juice today. Same thing with apple juice, for that matter. People think the best fruit is used, but it's actually the other way around. It was all about frugality. Still is."

Deb sees a potential culprit in the food-reform movement of the late 1800s. "They preached that refined foods should be avoided," she says. "And Marlborough pie depended upon sugar and flour." Warming to our search for a felon, I broach the subject of the temperance movement. Deb likes this tack. "Temperance advocates were gaining strength in New England in the mid-1800s," she says. "There were all kinds of ramifications for cookery. Before, a woman might have served pears poached in port, for both color and taste. By the mid-to-late 1800s, she was poaching them in beet juice. Maybe the same thing happened to our pudding. As you might imagine, without a bit of sherry, it just isn't the same."

I nod toward the pie, still resting on the secretary, and say something like, "I'll be the judge of that." Deb cuts me a slice. Turns out that a Marlborough pie commands your palate and announces its individuality with the same alacrity as a boiled-cider pie. I taste the tang of lemons, the silky musk of sherry, the bass register of apples. "If I had *my way,* this pie wouldn't be relegated to the Thanksgiving tables of foodways historians," Deb says. "It would be returned to its place of prominence on the New England table." My mouth is too full to tell her that she can have her way with me.

Marlborough Pie

In How America Eats, *Clementine Paddleford calls Marlborough pie "a glorification of everyday apple." I can think of no better moniker. Deb would agree too, on historical principles, for during the glory days of Marlborough pie, apples were thought to be nothing more than animal fodder. Only when gussied up by flour and sugar and other refined products, as in the making of a pie, were apples deemed edible by the middle class. One more thing: If you seek further glorification, serve this pie warm, in a puddle of chilled heavy cream or topped with a scoop of vanilla ice cream.*

CRUST

Use one of the recipes on pages 10, 20, or 39.

FILLING

- 1 lemon
- 3 large apples, peeled
- ½ tablespoon dry sherry
- 1 cup sugar
- 3 eggs
- ½ cup unsalted butter

(continued)

Squeeze the lemon into a large bowl. Grate the lemon peel into the same bowl, taking care to avoid the white pith. Grate the peeled apples coarsely and toss in as well. Pour in the sherry and stir in the sugar. Mix well. Beat the eggs until light. Cream the butter until soft and add the eggs, blending well. Stir the butter and egg mixture into the sweetened fruit.

FINISH

Heat the oven to 400°F. Roll the dough into two circles that are 2–3 inches wider in diameter than your pie shell or plate. Place one crust in the pie plate. Save the other crust for another use in the refrigerator. Lay the crust into the pie plate. Prick all over with a fork, and spoon in the pudding. Bake at 400°F for 15 minutes. Reduce heat to 350°F and bake 45 minutes, or until a knife inserted in the center comes out clean. Cool for at least 30 minutes before serving it warm.

Fidgeting with the Canon

i t's not easy to wrench myself from the time-capsule com-
forts of New England. And yet I must. I'm beginning to
ossify, to fix my palate and intellect in a time too long gone. I
seek a reentry without harrow, and find it in conversation
with Jasper White of Cambridge, Massachusetts, the dean of
neotraditionalist New England chefs.

At Summer Shack, his ode to New England shore fare,
White makes what he calls an Irish apple tart. Before we talk,
I eat a slice or two. His is a loose pie, baked flat on a sheet pan
instead of molded in a pie tin. It appears squat, kind of wild
and unkempt, as if the baker had laid the two-cruster in the
oven atop a turbo-powered lazy Susan and watched as cen-
trifugal force and convection rendered a ragged-edged and
toothsome pie.

I had hoped his take on apple pie would be more deviant.
But as you might expect from a student of the old ways,
White's pie was born of tradition. "I learned it when I was sev-
enteen," he tells me, "when I went to Ireland to live with my
grandparents. My aunt made one much like this. She never
used a pie plate. I tell people they were too poor to afford a
pie plate, but maybe it was just custom. Of course, they called
theirs a pie, same as we do. Only thing I've really changed is
calling it a tart. If I didn't, somebody would send it back.
They'd send it back and tell us what a real apple pie was."

Jasper White is not alone in cleaving to the old ways. I spent a good bit of time looking for chefs who fidget with the canonical apple pie. For the most part I failed. But I did encounter some pies—and some restauranteurs—you would do well to meet.

THIRTEEN

Taking Liberties

Soon after I signed the contract to write this book, my wife, Blair, arranged my fortieth-birthday dinner at Highlands Bar and Grill in Birmingham, Alabama. As has always been our experience at Frank Stitt's landmark restaurant, the meal—from *amuse-gueule* through shellfish platter, appetizer, and then entrée—was a triumph. But the dessert knocked our small band of revelers in the dirt. I remember it this way:

Out of the kitchen came a pretty, young

woman. On her uplifted arm she bore a gilt-edged mirror. Upon that mirror rested a collection of miniature apple pies. Walnuts and pecans were scattered about. Wedges of stinky blue cheese smoldered in two of the corners. Opposite each cheese stood silver chalices. One was filled with heavy cream, the other with glossy caramel. As she moved toward our table, candlelight spangled from the mirror and caromed off our brandy snifters. When she set the bright tableau down, I thought I might swoon. Granted, I was a mite intoxicated at that stage in the meal, but the effect was nevertheless stunning.

a t the time, I believed that I had achieved the apogee of apple pie. Though I had yet to travel much in support of my gleanings, and my hours among the library stacks had not cracked single digits, I thought that since I have eaten widely and well, and since I usually pay attention and take notes while eating, I had amassed a body of knowledge not likely to be compiled by most apple pie–loving mortals.

In assembling a roster of potential research areas, I had devised two categories: home cooks and restaurant chefs. I did not fall prey to the rarefied attitude that prevented my friend the North Carolina attorney from recognizing the genius of Karen Barker, but I did err when I figured that my categorization of pie might be illuminating. Luckily, I've learned a little over the course of the past year.

I now know that in the matter of apple pie chefs tend to

stay their hands after a minor fillip. The truly innovative pie is often the product of home bakers like Cindy Deal who rely upon Red Hots, or the unknown baker who, faced with a shortage of fruit, imagined the first mock apple pie. Now, when I recollect that dessert from Highlands, I think no less of it. (I can still recall how a spot of smoky-sweet caramel punctuated a forkful of pie and Roquefort.) Instead, I recognize it as a particularly well-executed take on a wholly traditional dish.

And yet I can't quite shake my faith in the possibility of transcendental and transformational restaurant pie. In the waning months of my research, I make one last attempt. Rumor has it that GW Fins, a seafood restaurant in New Orleans's French Quarter, serves an apple pie with a cheese-straw crust. I confirm this by telephone, and rather than stop to analyze the potential, I drive south.

tenney Flynn and I sit in a corner booth in GW Fins. It's midafternoon. The dinner crush is still a few hours away. Somehow I had pictured a small place run by a chef who divines the menu each morning and serves posh dishes to a white-shoe clientele. But Flynn's restaurant, set in what was once the parking garage of an old-line New Orleans department store, cranks out two or three hundred covers a night. Granted, those are not Summer Shack numbers, but the volume is impressive—especially when you consider that forty of those diners are likely to eat a baked-to-order apple pie.

One of those pies, set on a round of china, sits between us, cooling on the napped tabletop. It's a six-incher, slightly domed, with a crust somewhere between orange and brown. Flynn, a tightly coiled man with a close-cropped beard, cuts it in half. In the gap, he places a scoop of ice cream, which quickly becomes a puddle. I sink my fork into the pie and drag it through the cream as Tenney explains the genesis of his cheese-straw crust.

I know, upon first bite, that this is not a canon-blaster of a pie. The crust is not even a riff on a cheese straw, it *is* a cheese straw. Flynn scratches at his beard and tells me that was the point. "I grew up with cheese straws," he says. "They were party food, church basement food, covered-dish food. I made money at Christmas by picking shells off the ground for my mother to use when she made those wafer-style ones, the ones where you put a pecan in the center."

I dig a little, searching for a technique or a twist that was not born in the home kitchen. I find plenty. Flynn works with two crusts: The bottom one is suffused with lard; the top one is, in essence, the cheese-straw recipe from *Bill Neal's Southern Cooking*. He also cooks the apples down like a strudel and, in the manner of many a restaurant chef inclined to eschew caloric concerns in favor of flavor, stokes them with heavy cream.

But when I try to frame his apple pie within the context of restaurant-born creativity, Flynn swings the conversation back around to home, to family. "My grandparents were farmers in West Virginia," he tells me. "I took my son up there not long ago. We went down in the old root cellar. It smelled like my grandmother, like apples and kraut. To tell you the truth, it made me think of apple pie."

i n *Fried Chicken: An American Story,* I write of a Southern chef who brines his chicken in sweet tea before he fries it. Now that's what I call a substantive reworking of an iconic American dish. When confronting apple pie, chefs—like Tenney Flynn and Jasper White and most everyone else I meet—bake in a way that is comparatively hidebound. Sure, they might gussy up the presentation. And yes, I've seen some untoward things done with phyllo. But no one appears to succeed at taking grand liberties with the national dessert.

Depending upon my mood and the last pie I have tasted, I read this phenomenon in different ways: Perhaps the elemental apple pie, whether it be a sliced apple standard or a puree of the kind I discovered in Vermont and Massachusetts, is recognized by chefs as perfection achieved. Or maybe apple pie is like barbecue. Chefs are fearful of toying with it because they know that sentimental familiarity usually trumps all in the case of this dish. Or American identity and apple pie have become intertwined to the point that chefs risk the ire of their public when they rework the culinary equivalent of motherhood's dowry.

Cheese-Straw Apple Pie

Though Tenney Flynn flirted with the idea of sharing his full recipe with me, I let the matter drop because Blair wanted to have a go at it. Lord knows she was up to the task of anything involving cheese straws, for, early in our marriage, I grew accustomed to retiring for bed on the eve of a party while she remained in the kitchen, working a pastry gun like an Uzi, strafing the counter with strips of cayenne-red dough. Her recipe, by the way, is far simpler than what I learned of his. I won't say that it's better. I will say that it's a masterstroke.

CRUST

- 1½ sticks unsalted butter, cut into small pieces
- 2 tablespoons cold vegetable shortening, cut into pieces
- 3 cups all-purpose flour
- 1 teaspoon salt
- 1 or 2 teaspoon(s) cayenne pepper
- 2⅓ cups shredded extra-sharp cheddar cheese
- ½ cup plus 2 tablespoons ice water

Frigidity is all-important here. Place butter and short-ening in freezer for at least an hour before mixing. Pulse flour, salt, and cayenne pepper in food processor. Remove the lid and tuck the butter and shortening into the mixture. Pulse the machine 4 times to cut in the butter. Add 1⅓ cups of cheese and pulse 4 more times. Sprinkle half of the water over the flour mixture and pulse 5 or 6 times. Add the rest of the water and pulse 5 or 6 more times, until the pastry looks like very coarse crumbs.

Move mixture to a chilled bowl and work until dough is formed. Round into two balls, one slightly larger than the other. Wrap each dough ball in two layers of plastic wrap and press them into disks. Chill at least three hours.

FILLING

- 5 large, tart apples
- ½ large lemon
- ½ cup dark brown sugar
- 1 tablespoon all-purpose flour
- 1 teaspoon cinnamon
- 1 teaspoon vanilla
- ½ teaspoon salt

(continued)

- ¼ teaspoon freshly ground nutmeg
- 1½ tablespoons butter, cut into six parts

Heat oven to 400°F. Peel and slice apples. In a bowl, mix the apples, lemon juice, dark brown sugar, flour, cinnamon, vanilla, salt, and nutmeg with your hands. Set aside and retrieve the piecrusts from the refrigerator.

FINISH

Roll the dough into two circles that are 2–3 inches wider in diameter than your pie shell or plate. Press the bottom crust into the pie plate and mound apples until they fill the crust and dome slightly. Scatter the butter over the mound. Cut a center vent the size of a dime into the top crust. Sprinkle the remaining cup of shredded cheese onto the crust. With a rolling pin, roll lightly to press the cheese into the dough. Roll the crust onto the rolling pin so that the rolling pin resembles the sausage in a pig-in-a-blanket. Unroll the crust, cheese-side down, on top of the apples. Bake at 400°F for 10 minutes. Reduce the heat to 350°F and bake for 40 to 50 minutes longer. Crimp the edges of the crusts.

Crumbs in His Beard

Consider the phrase "as American as apple pie." And then join me in expending a bit of intellectual energy to establish how and why apple pie came to be a proxy for American identity.

The phrase seems to have entered into vogue during the early years of the twentieth century. Among the first references I came across was a 1930 newspaper account wherein an Ohio churchman's refusal to recognize the failure of Prohibition was deemed "as typically American as apple pie." Earlier was a 1921 profile of Alice Gentle, a contralto with Chicago's Ravinia Opera, who foretold the coming of a native opera that would be "as American as apple pie, wheat cakes, corn on the cob, barbecues, Mississippi River steamboats, one-night stands, and mail-order houses."

The idea that such an expression was popularized during the years following the tumult of the First World War makes good sense to me, for out of tempest often comes a cohesive impulse or slogan. ("Remember the Alamo!" "Remember the *Maine*!" "Turn on, tune in, drop out!") In that same vein, there exists more than one tale wherein wartime president Abraham Lincoln coined the phrase.

One of the most frequently cited Lincoln stories is set in Burkittsville, Maryland. The year is 1862. On his way home from visiting the battlefield at Antietam, Lincoln's carriage breaks down. While it is being repaired at a local tannery, the presidential party eats lunch on the veranda of a nearby home. And when a woman who lives up the street brings over a fresh-from-the-oven pie, Lincoln supposedly remarks, "Nothing is as American as apple pie."

FOURTEEN

To Hell with Tarte Tatin!

abraham Lincoln is said to have developed a taste for apple pie while still a young lawyer. Natives of New Salem, Illinois, boast that when he departed for the White House, the ladies of their town banded together to keep him in pies, shipping his favorites to Washington on a regular basis. But these were no ordinary pies. According to contemporary accounts, the ladies cut stars for steam vents and incised various letters into the crusts. An L signified the pie was intended for the president himself; an A denoted that apples lay beneath.

Of course, George Washington is perennially associated with cherry trees. The knowledge that cherry trees beget cherries which in turn beget cherry pies could be part of the reason that few glom on to the story that William Ainsworth Porter, Washington's cook during the Revolutionary War, is responsible for rendering apple pie a symbol of American identity. No matter the strength of Porter's claim, there is little doubt that apple pie was a White House constant.

In 1887, Hugo Ziemann, steward of the White House, published *The White House Cookbook: Cooking, Toilet and Household Recipes, Menus, Dinner-Giving, Table Etiquette, Care of the Sick, Health Suggestions, Facts Worth Knowing, Etc., Etc.: A Cyclopedia of Information for the Home.* Contained within were four recipes for apple-custard pie, one for mock apple pie (with Boston crackers), one for green-apple pie, one for Irish apple pie (with quince marmalade), and one for apple and peach meringue pie. If that cornucopia of recipes wasn't enough to catch the eye of a baker in the market for a book, the preface proclaimed that Ziemann was once a "caterer for that Prince Napoleon who was killed while fighting the Zulus of Africa."

What remains unclear is when apple pie crossed over—when it ceased being just a dessert and took on its role as fulcrum for all manner of nationalistic bluster and electoral aspirations. By 1927, the British recognized the message lurking between the crusts. "American pie breeds dyspepsia, dyspepsia breeds restlessness, and restlessness begets a feverish but nonetheless formidable material progress," declared an editorial in the London *Evening News*. "The American apple pie is the sheer gastronomic equivalent of an incendiary bomb."

I'm sure the crossover had taken place by the time Henrietta Nesbitt was employed as the cook for President and Mrs. Roosevelt. She worked at the height of the Depression, at a time when apple pie came to be seen as an everyman's dish, equally suitable for the Civilian Conservation Corps worker and the chief executive. In other words, she cooked for the president at a time when apple pie possessed a peculiar emotional resonance, when many were going hungry, when many struggled to understand how such a symbol of America could reflect the poverty-engendered frugality of the day, and, at the very same time, foretell our eventual deliverance.

The party-line story was that Nesbitt—famous for baking in her hometown of Hyde Park, New York—earned the fidelity of the Roosevelts by shipping apple pies to the future president while he was still governor of New York. And then, on the strength of those same pies, Eleanor Roosevelt invited her to be the general housekeeper at the White House, responsible for planning meals and managing a staff of more than thirty. Come to think of it, Nesbitt's story sounds suspiciously like the one told of Lincoln's hometown bake-and-ship ladies.

n̲o matter the date of said crossover, there can be little doubt that it occurred. We now live in an age when every morsel that issues forth from the White House kitchen is not only well cooked but well considered.

Nowadays dessert is détente. When the president of Ireland comes to dinner at the White House, the finale is a cookie-dough castle adorned with a green harp. The president of Greece gets a dessert framed in Ionic columns crafted from white chocolate. When the president of Chile arrives to discuss free trade, he is presented with a faux crate, crafted of sugar and painted with food coloring to resemble wood. PRODUCE OF CHILE is stamped on the side, also with food coloring. And the crate is filled with lemon sherbet molded in the form of white asparagus, and lime sherbet molded in the form of green asparagus.

Roland Mesnier is the French-born pastry chef formerly responsible for these grand state-dinner desserts. He served five presidents, beginning with Jimmy Carter, whose wife, Rosalynn, secured his American citizenship. Though a recent *New York Times* article described him as "utterly French in outlook and manner," it is obvious that the reporter never asked Mesnier his opinions about our national dessert.

i do. We meet in the lobby of the Hotel Washington, catercorner from the White House. Mesnier looks and sounds Gallic, in the manner of a late-career Gérard Depardieu. But Mesnier's opinions on pie could not be more American.

"Apple pie is one of my specialties," he tells me. "I saw my first one in Bermuda and I was immediately impressed. It was exciting. I said to myself, 'Here is a dessert.' It's simple, there's no point to break heads over it, but it's not as simple as you think. . . . I consider myself a student of pie. I read recipes and study techniques. But you can't follow an apple pie recipe exactly. You've got to go with the flow, go with the apples."

By the time we talk of tarte Tatin, he is gesticulating wildly. "The one thing I can't abide is how the French keep Frenchifying everything," he says, his voice rising, his *r*'s trilling. "Tarte Tatin and apple pie are nothing alike. In a tarte Tatin, the apples are mere ghosts. The French say Americans are taking over their country, their cuisine. And I see them trying to do the same when they claim apple pie." He's convincing, animated, entertaining. "The apple pie belongs to the American housewife," he says. "This is mom's. I've just borrowed it for a bit."

I break in to ask the obvious question: "So what do you do with apple pie when you borrow it? Say, for a state dinner?" Mesnier does not answer directly. I can't tell whether he's too excited to focus or whether he's avoiding the question. What follows is a personal disquisition on apple pie during which Mesnier bemoans the tendency of chefs to overseason, "emptying every spice in the cabinet into their pies," and praises Crisco as a solution to "soggy crusts that turn out like pasta."

And then he unfurls his masterpiece. In the waning days of the Clinton administration, Mesnier concocted an apple-pie dessert for a dinner honoring state governors. "The image was that of a pie with a kitchen towel draped over it," recalls the chef. "There was one for every table. I silk-screened cocoa powder on a crumpled sheet of phyllo dough to make it look like a kitchen towel. And we spun red apples out of sugar and mounted those behind each pie. When it came time to serve, butlers passed through the room and offered pies. The guests helped themselves to a slice and a scoop of honey ice cream."

I look up from my note-taking to eye Mesnier. I compose his scene in my head. I contemplate the occasion when mom's apple pie reached fullest flower in the hands of a lapsed Frenchman. And I recall research done in preparation for my interview with Mesnier, about how, during the election of 1840, Whig political boss Thurlow Weed incorporated a national prejudice against "fancy French dining" in William Henry Harrison's Log Cabin campaign. Weed claimed that incumbent Martin Van Buren employed a French chef in the White House and had a taste for cookery that befitted a monarch rather than a man of the people. The Whig Harrison was, according to Weed, a compatriot of the commoner who subsisted on a frontier diet of "raw beef and salt."

I catch myself. I know I'm overintellectualizing this. I conjure Mesnier's dining room scene again. I visualize the pies, the towels, the apples. My mouth waters. My cynicism fades. My country, 'tis of thee.

White House Pie

White House Pie is not to be confused with "house pie," a term from the early years of our republic. House pie was made from whatever might be lying about the house. It was not a dessert with a stellar reputation. "House pie, in country places, is made from apples neither peeled nor freed from their core," wrote a Swedish minister in a 1758 account of the settling of Maryland. "And its crust is not broken if a wagon wheel rolls over it." This recipe, based in part on instructions dictated to me by Roland Mesnier, comes out a bit better.

CRUST

Use one of the recipes on pages 10, 20, or 39.

FILLING

- 5 apples, peeled, cored and cut into chunks (Mesnier likes Honey Crisps, a newer variety grown in Virginia.)
- 5 tablespoons butter
- 5 tablespoons sugar, plus 1 tablespoon for sprinkling across the top crust
- 1 teaspoon cinnamon

(continued)

- 2 teaspoons lemon juice
- 2 tablespoons cake crumbs (or plain bread crumbs)
- ¼ cup raisins

Toss apples in a skillet with butter, sugar, cinnamon, and lemon juice. Cook over medium-high heat for about 10 minutes, or until the apples begin to brown ever so slightly. Cool the mixture for 15 minutes. Pour the apples and the juice into a bowl. Add the cake crumbs or bread crumbs and the raisins to soak up the juices.

FINISH

Heat the oven to 375°F. Lay down the bottom crust. Spoon in the filling. Lay on the top crust and crimp. Cut a center steam vent. Bake 15 minutes at 375°F. Reduce the heat to 350F° and bake for 40 minutes or until the top crust is golden. Serve warm with ice cream or crème fraîche.

Of Pie I Sing

b lair, my wife, argued for a different title
for this book. She thought *Apple Pie: A
Love Story* was better. She pointed out that seduction animates any good love affair. Just as
anxiety propels. And rejection throttles. She
told me that I experienced all three while writing and researching this book. Sometimes in
one day.

I've known seduction. I've stood in a storefront bakery in Albuquerque and listened to a

man named Señor Pie lay down a line worthy of Barry White, a line about how a great slice of pie "scoots out from beneath the bedsheets and shows its stuff." I've mused that apple pie may well be a seductress, albeit the kind that dresses in plaid flannel and flashes the barest hint of thigh. I've even seen clear to parlay such thought into a Web search that turned up www.apple-pie-entertainment.com, an outfit advertising the "finest exotic dancers in New England."

Rejection was a constant. I could stop upon recounting my experience at the Great American Pie Festival in Celebration. I still shiver when I conjure that roadway slush lying prostrate on my mind's palate. I still flee when I see somebody approaching on a Segway. But if I want to understand true rejection, I need only recollect the tale of Margo Hayes, the fried-pie queen whose husband gave *her* tomatoes to *his* hussy.

In her mention of anxiety, however, Blair may have come closest to defining my search for meaning amidst the crusts. At the root of my anxiety was a single question: Could I get it right? In other words, could I draft a portrait of America by pie that avoided sentimentality while it showcased rawboned emotion and honest patriotic expression?

few of the people I met articulated why apple pie is American. Fewer still told me how or why it has come to symbolize a blithe land of manicured *Leave It to Beaver* lawns and well-crimped crusts. But almost everyone liked to talk of pie.

I've tried to give those people voice. I met most across a table set with knife and fork and pie plate. I shared a banquette with one at a hotel across the street from the White House. Another fed me pie on a California mountaintop. Others I discovered among the stacks, between the covers of abolitionist manifestos and gardening books and lesbian newsletters. Others still—like the Shaker men who invented the apple corer and the Shaker women who devised an early convection oven—eluded my grasp.

After a bit of reflection and distillation, I've come to believe that they told me two things: Apple pie is born of frugality, they said. And apple pie is alchemical.

I learned of frugality from a Vermont man who makes boiled cider from windfall fruit. And from his wife, who baked me an ascetic and delicious pie for Saturday breakfast. I talked of root cellars full of apples with an Iowa farmwife. I talked of milkshakes made of cast-off slices with an Iowa grill cook. I talked with a Massachusetts scholar about the proper way to filter worms and flotsam from the makings of a Marlborough pie.

In the end, it was the everyday alchemy that turned my head: mornings that began with a sack of flour and a pile of apples and reached their apogee when someone—most often my wife—pulled a sugar-shellacked pie from an oven and set it on a trivet to cool. In that moment of promise, as cinnamon vapors spiraled from the steam vents and candied apple juice sought a gap in the crimp, I fell in love all over again with apple pie. In that alchemy I found fidelity, allegiance, identity. And I knew that all the saccharine sentiment and jingoism in the world could not sway me. Apple pie still matters as a symbol of home, a totem of American bounty.

Thoughts on Technique,
Ingredients, and Equipment
& My Little Black Book of Pie

this book offers two different ways to get your apple-pie fix. If you're keen on making your own, read on for a few tips on technique. Or, if you'd rather gas up the car and go barreling across America in search of a great pastry, skip to page 155, where I offer a roster of bakers and bakeries worthy of a pilgrimage.

Technique

Whoever coined the expression "easy as pie" was either an innately talented baker or a liar. If you have never baked a pie, the word "easy" will not come to mind as you roll out that first crust. Chances are, it will tear. And it will turn out lopsided. And if you're making a two-crust pie, juices will surely breach the crimp and splatter about your oven.

But have faith. Prospects will brighten. Your third crust will likely approximate a circle. And your fourth crust may boast sufficient integrity to survive a stretch across that mound of apples. By crust five, your hands will know what your eyes may never comprehend.

Of course, that's the point: In the matter of pie, tactile knowledge beats eyeballing or book learning. So if you're new to the practice of apple pie, devote an hour or more to a crust clinic. Flour, after all, is cheap.

Now that you're girded for the struggle, you should know my prejudices.

Crust

To my mind and palate, crust is key. Although I am not one of those benighted souls who considers the filling to be nothing more than a condiment for the crust, I do believe that no filling can rescue a bad crust. On pages 10, 20, 39, 78, and 134, I offer five different crust recipes. If you desire more recipes or more detailed instruction, try Karen Barker's *Sweet Stuff* or Rose Levy Beranbaum's *Pie and Pastry Bible.* Both are useful for aspiring bakers.

You will find no lattice-crust pies between these pages. No matter how carefully I cut them, lattice-crust slices always seem to fall apart before I can ferry them to my mouth. And although I can live with a crumb topping, the little lumps of butter and sugar and flour remind me of gravel. And I don't like gravel on my pie.

Last, a confession: We all succumb once in a while. If you must use a prefab piecrust, forgo those frozen pie-plate versions for the pricey but good refrigerator case piecrusts made by Pillsbury. As for flour, my wife and I prefer White Lily.

Apples

Grocery-store apples get a bad rap. Novelist Jack Butler once wrote that they have "all the fiber of a politician's moral courage, all the flavor of a C.E.O.'s reading habits." For the most part, he's right. If you have access to locally grown heirloom variety apples, by all means use them. If you want to learn more about heirloom varieties, pick up the massive *Old Southern Apples* by Creighton Lee Calhoun or *Apples: A Catalogue of International Varieties* by Thomas Burford.

But the reality is that Americans tend to be grocery-store buyers. Fortunately, grocers are getting smarter. Insipid Red Delicious apples are losing bin space to spicy Braeburns, tangy Pink Ladies, and juicy Cameos. All are good baking apples, and all are showing up with regularity at even the big-box retailers. Of course, if all else fails, tart Granny Smiths are omnipresent and well suited to baking.

Equipment

Invest in a ceramic or Pyrex pie plate. The Pyrex version allows you the opportunity to gauge, with a quick peek, the color of your bottom crust. You might also want to purchase a pie collar, a circular metal thingy that will shield the crust edges from burning. (Or just fashion a collar from strips of aluminum foil.)

Serving

As a rule, don't cut a pie until it has rested for at least an hour. If you cut a pie too early, the juices will seep out into the void left by the slice. And never—ever—put a pie in the refrigerator. Your masterpiece will dry out. What's more, it will emerge smelling like its shelf mates. (Anchovy pizza and apple pie are not simpatico.)

Apple pie will keep, covered, for two days on your counter. If it lasts more than two days, it's probably sub-par pie anyway. Resist the urge to heat a slice in the microwave. Those machines are the ruination of a well-made crust. Instead, tent your slice with foil and heat it in a conventional oven. Of late, I've grown particularly fond of refreshing day-old pie by pouring on a glug of chilled cream.

Want to Learn More?

If you pine for more apple-pie recipes, try Ken Haedrich's book *Apple Pie Perfect: 100 Delicious and Decidedly Different Recipes for America's Favorite Pie*. Want to learn more about apple history? I heartily recommend *Apples* by Frank Browning, a personal history entwined with pomological insights.

My Little Black Book of Apple Pie

NORTHEAST

Bread Line
1751 Pennsylvania Avenue
Washington, DC
202-822-8900

City Bakery
3 West 18th Street
New York, NY
212-366-1414

Old Sturbridge Village
Route 20
Sturbridge, MA
508-347-3362

Old Tavern at Grafton
92 Main Street
Grafton, VT
802-843-2231

Burnham Hollow Country
    Store
Route 4
Rutland, VT
802-773-8830

Summer Shack
149 Alewife Brook Parkway
Cambridge, MA
617-520-9500

Woods Cider Mill
1482 Weathersfield Center
   Road
Weathersfield, VT
802-263-5547

SOUTHEAST

Early Girl
8 Wall Street
Asheville, NC
828-259-9292

GW Fin's
808 Bienville Street
New Orleans, LA
504-581-3467

Highlands Bar and Grill
2011 11th Avenue South
Birmingham, AL
205-939-1400

Jerry Kendall's Fruit Market
1118 South 1st Street
Union City, TN
731-884-0002

Margo's Country Store
23260 Highway 412 East
Parsons, TN
731-845-5281

Magnolia Grill
1002 9th Street
Durham, NC
919-286-3609

MIDWEST

Deal's Orchard
1102 244th Street
Jefferson, IA
515-386-8279

Hamburg Inn #2
214 North Linn Street
Iowa City, IA
319-337-5512

WEST

Big Y Café
9656 North Road
Peshastin, WA
509-548-5012

Home Fires Bakery
13013 Bayne Road
Leavenworth, WA
509-548-7362

Janie's Pie Factory
1832 Nacogdoches Road
San Antonio, TX
210-826-8715

Julian Pie Company
2225 Main Street
Julian, CA
760-765-2449

Lone Pine Fruit and Espresso
23041 Highway 97
Orondo, WA
509-682-1514

Señor Pie
6431 Gibson Boulevard, S.E.
Albuquerque, NM
505-255-1602

Tootie Pie
455 Stringtown Road
Medina, TX
830-589-2994

Acknowledgments

My wife, Blair, baked every last one of these pies. And I do mean *every last one*. I realize that it's customary to pay homage to one's spouse in the acknowledgments, but Blair's participation in this project was anything but pro forma. I am in her debt and under her spell.

Many of the people who helped me get their due in the text. The following is a list of those who don't:

Lance Elko at *Attaché* gave me ink. (One of the essays herein originally appeared therein.) Franklin Williams and Beckett Howorth and Andy Harper and Dorothy Howorth tested recipes and offered insights. Pableaux Johnson offered excellent leads. Sandy Oliver of *Food History News* shared scholarship, as did John Rees. Jill Buchanan offered a berth and a road map. Square Books stocked my library. Maya and Jimmy Kennedy fed me well. William Thomas got me drunk. John Long turned on the radio in Cleveland. Thomas Head and Billy Gottshall and Mark Furstenberg and Joan Nathan and Matt McMillen gave me the keys to the capital. Ari Weinzweig inspired me with tales of old cheese. Frank Stitt and pastry chef Amanda Culver engineered an apple-pie summit at Highlands. Becky Mercuri scoured the Web. Ed Levine was a spy in the house of pie. Anissa Mack conjured a world I never saw, a pie I never tasted.

Robb Walsh housed me and instructed me in the ways of

Texas. Matt and Anne Konigsmark housed me and instructed me in the ways of New Orleans. Corby Kummer fed me Boston. William Woys Weaver offered entrée to the Pennsylvania Dutch. The good folks at Prairie Lights in Iowa City endured questions and offered Iowa insights. So did Matt and Ted Lee. Susan Puckett paved the way with Red Hots. Barbara Kuck hauled out a motherlode of books when I visited the Johnson and Wales archives. Bill and Cheryl Alters Jamison feted me in Santa Fe. Ronni Lundy taught me about fried pies.

Mary Beth Lasseter managed my e-mail and me. John Egerton offered wise counsel. Colleagues at the Southern Foodways Alliance gave me the time to eat and read and write. Devin Cox turned out two brilliant cover designs on a dime. Amy Evans baked a pie, wrangled a child, and shot great pics. David Black leaned back in his chair and invited me to imagine what might be. Rich Florest was ever gracious and kind. And Jennifer Hershey proved wrong all the wags who say editors don't edit anymore.

About the Author

John T. Edge writes frequently for *Gourmet, Saveur, Attaché,* and other publications. He was a longtime columnist for the *Oxford American.* His work is featured in the 2001 through 2004 editions of the *Best Food Writing* compilation. He was a finalist for the 2004 M. F. K. Fisher Distinguished Writing Award from the James Beard Foundation.

He has a number of books to his credit, including the James Beard Award–nominated cookbook, *A Gracious Plenty: Recipes and Recollections from the American South,* and *Southern Belly,* a mosaic-like portrait of southern food told through profiles of people and places. He is general editor of the book series *Cornbread Nation: The Best of Southern Food Writing* and foodways section editor for the forthcoming edition of the *Encyclopedia of Southern Culture.*

Edge, who holds a master's degree in Southern studies from the University of Mississippi, is director of the Southern Foodways Alliance, an institute of the Center for the Study of Southern Culture at the University of Mississippi, where he dedicates his time to studying, celebrating, promoting, and preserving the diverse food cultures of America.

Edge is one of the founders and principals of the Civil Rights Commemoration Initiative, which is working to install a civil rights movement memorial at the University of Mississippi. In 2003, he was named "One of Twenty Southerners to Watch" by the *Financial Times* of London. The award recognizes "Southerners whose achievements will have a greater impact in the future, both on the national and international stage."

Edge lives in Oxford, Mississippi, with his son, Jess, and his wife, Blair Hobbs, a teacher and painter. His website is www.johntedge.com.